LIVING
IN TH[E...]

A guide to inexpensive living and making money in the Land of Lakes and Volcanoes

Written by
CHRISTOPHER HOWARD

® ALL RIGHTS RESERVED - TODOS DERECHOS RESERVADOS

LIVING AND INVESTING IN THE NEW NICARAGUA

By Christopher Howard

First Edition

First Edition, published in Costa Rica

© 2001-2002 Editora de Turismo Nacional, S.A.

ISBN 1-881233-50-2

**Costa Rica Books
Suite 1 SJO 981
P.O. Box 025216
Miami, FL 33102-5216
www.liveinnicaragua.com
www.costaricabooks.com
www.amazon.com**

ALL RIGHTS RESERVED. No part of this book may be reproduced without written permission of the authors and copyright owner.

TODOS DERECHOS RESERVADOS. Esta publicación está protegida por las disposiciones legales de impresión y derechos de autor. Queda prohibido cualquier tipo de reproducción, grabación o fotocopiado sin permiso escrito de los autores.

"Si la patria es pequeña, uno grande la sueña."

"If a country is small, one dreams of it as big."

Rubén Darío
Nicaraguan Poet

ACKNOWLDGEMENTS

This edition would not have become a reality without the invaluable help of many people.

I would first like to thank my assistant Mary de Waal in the U.S. for her invaluable help. She is truly a jewel. Also my graphic designer, William "El Mago" Morales, for his hard work and patience.

A special thanks to the following people in Granada and Costa Rica for their contributions to this edition: Sandy Perkoff, Lance Carlson, Jay Trettien, Bill Harper, Rob Hodel, Dr. Daniel Spitzer and many more.

I am indebted to Diego Congote and Martha Luz G. de Barrios from The Nicaraguan Institute of Tourism for all of the information and invaluable resources and contacts they provided.

Also I would like to mention all of the useful information the U.S. Embassy in Managua contributed to this book.

I would like to acknowledge all of the help I have received from the Publishers Marketing Association's and Amazon.com's programs for independent publishers. Thanks to them, this book is now available in the U.S., Canada and rest of the world.

Finally, I would like to express my eternal gratitude to members of my family, especially my late mother, for their constant support when I needed it the most.

Christopher Howard
San José, Costa Rica

MORE ABOUT THE AUTHOR

Christopher Howard has resided in Central America for over fifteen years and is a Costa Rican citizen.

During this time he has had the opportunity to gather a plethora of information about living, investing and retiring in Costa Rica and the rest of Central America. It is not surprising that he has first-hand knowledge of and insight into all aspects of the region's culture and its people. Because of his expertise he is a frequent lecturer for the Investors Club of Costa Rica.

Mr. Howard has an extensive foreign language background, having earned a B.A. in Latin American studies and a Master's degree in Spanish from the University of California. He also has credentials to teach Spanish at all levels from California State University, San Francisco.

Howard was the recipient of scholarships for graduate study at the University of the Americas in Puebla, Mexico, and

The author in front of his new home in Lagunilla de Heredia.

the Jesuit University of Guadalajara, Mexico in conjunction with the University of San Diego, California. He has written three foreign language books including the best-selling *Costa Rican Spanish Survival Course* and, in 1985, founded a successful language institute in San José, Costa Rica.

At present, Chris Howard has been busy leading monthly relocation tours for people thinking of moving to Costa Rica; working as a paid consultant for *National Geographic Magazine*; putting the finishing touches on a book about Costa Rican idioms; publishing articles for several on-line publications for potential expatriates and working on a feature action movie script to be filmed in Central America.

In 1999 Mr. Howard published the visionary guidebook, "*Living and Investing in the 'New' Cuba.*"

CONTENTS

FOREWORD xiii

CHAPTER I

NICARAGUA'S LAND, HISTORY AND PEOPLE 1
   THE LAY OF THE LAND 1
   MAPS 3-4
   WEATHER 5
   WHERE TO LIVE IN NICARAGUA 5
   A GREAT ONE-OF-A-KIND TOUR 16
   NICARAGUA'S HISTORY IN BRIEF 18
   GOVERNMENT 21
   ECONOMY 21
   THE PEOPLE 23

CHAPTER II

SAVING MONEY IN NICARAGUA 29
   HOW MUCH DOES IT COST TO LIVE IN
   NICARAGUA? 29
   TIPPING 32
   AFFORDABLE HIRED HELP 33
   HEALTH CARE 44
      Staying Healthy 44
      Dental Care 47
      Pharmacies 46
      Cosmetic Surgery... 49
      Doctor's List 49
      Care for the Elderly 50
   MONEY 50
   BANKING 51
   TAXES 52
   TAX PROTECTION... 59
   FORMING A PANAMANIAN CORPORATION 62
   INSURANCE 65

CHAPTER III

MAKING MONEY IN NICARAGUA	67
INVESTING IN NICARAGUA	67
The Tourism Boom	73
Opportunities	74
Minor Obstacles to Doing Business	75
NICARAGUA'S NASCENT STOCK MARKET	79
REAL ESTATE INVESTMENTS	80
Rentals	80
General Advice When Buying Real Estate in Central America	82
Building A Home…	84
Speculating	84
Rules for Buying Property in Nicaragua…	85
Steps to Buying and Registering Land	85
Real Estate Taxes	86
Home Insurance	86
Special Considerations for Tourism Projects	86
Special Considerations for Foreign Investors	86
FINDING WORK IN COSTA RICA	88
STARTING A BUSINESS	90
OCCASIONAL ROADBLOCKS TO DOING BUSNIESS IN NICARAGUA..	95
COMMON BUSINESS SENSE IN NICARAGUA	96

CHAPTER IV

RED TAPE	**101**
DEALING WITH BUREAUCRACY IN LATIN AMERICA..	101
HOW TO BECOME A LEGAL RESIDENT OF NICARAGUA	107
IMMIGRATION AND OTHER MATTERS	111
SHIPPING AN AUTOMOBILE OR HOUSEHOLD GOODS TO NICARAGUA	113
DRIVING A CAR TO NICARAGUA	116

HOW TO FIND A LAWYER 117
FOREIGN EMBASSIES AND CONSULATES
IN NICARAGUA 121
NICARAGUAN CONSULATES ABROAD.........................122

CHAPTER V

STAYING BUSY AND HAPPY IN NICARAGUA.........................125
    SOME SOUND ADVICE..125
    BOOKS, MAGAZINES AND NEWSPAPERS 126
    TELEVISION AND RADIO 128
    VIDEO RENTALS 130
    SHOPPING..130
    NICARAGUAN PASTIMES..133
    MUSEUMS AND ART GALLERIES..................................134
    A PARADISE FOR WATERSPORTS
    AND NATURE LOVERS...135
    BASEBALL IN NICARAGUA..136
    WHERE TO MAKE FRIENDS 137
    LOVE AND PERMANENT COMPANIONSHIP 139
    NIGHTLIFE AND ENTERTAINMENT................................145
    GAMBLING 147
    MOVIES AND THEATERS IN NICARAGUA 147

CHAPTER VI

COMMUNICATIONS 149
    TELEPHONE AND INTERNET SERVICES..........................149
    MAIL SERVICE 152
    RECEIVING MONEY FROM ABROAD 154

CHAPTER VII

EDUCATION 157
    HOW TO LEARN SPANISH...157
    NICARAGUA'S INSTITUTIONS OF
    HIGHER LEARNING...166
    PRIVATE ELEMENTARY AND

HIGH SCHOOLS 167

CHAPTER VIII

GETTING AROUND 171
    AIR TRAVEL TO, IN AND AROUND NICARAGUA 171
    TRAVELING BY BUS IN NICARAGUA 172
    BUS TRAVEL TO AND FROM NICARAGUA 174
    NICARAGUA'S TAXIS 174
    AUTOMOBILE RENTALS 176
    DRIVING IN NICARAGUA 177
    TRAVELING BY BOAT 181
    KEEPING YOUR BEARINGS STRAIGHT 181

CHAPTER IX

MORE USUEFUL INFORMATION 183
AFFORDABLE FOODS 183
    NICARAGUA'S HOLIDAYS 188
    RELIGION 189
    BRINGING YOUR PETS TO NICARAGUA 189
    UNDERSTANDING THE METRIC SYSTEM 191

CHAPTER X

PARTING THOUGHTS AND ADVICE 193
    PERSONAL SAFETY IN NICARAGUA 193
    LIFE AS AN EXPATRIATE 196
    ADDITIONALSOURCES OF INFORMATION
    ABOUT LIVING IN NICARAGUA 200
    SUGGESTED READING 203
    IMPORTANT SPANISH PHRASES
    AND VOCABULARY 205
    IMPORTANT CONTACTS 209
    IMPORTANT PHONE NUMBERS 227
    INDEX 230

FOREWORD

WHY NICARAGUA?

Our answer, is "Why Not?" Located in the heart of Central America, Nicaragua is an exceptional country with its spectacular lakes, towering volcanoes, friendly people and legendary towns filled with cultural richness. The country beckons foreigners to come and see all it has to offer.

Some foreigners have already gotten wind of the country's potential. A recent article in USA Today states that over 5,000 Americans currently call Nicaragua their home.

Devastated by the wrath of mother nature, its tumultuous political past, and a streak of misfortune, the country is now poised to emerge as a travel hot-spot, a potential haven for expatriates and a place where unlimitied opportunities await the energetic entrpreneur.

In the 1980s most of Central American including Nicaragua was ground zero in the cold war, with the Soviets, Cubans and U.S. orchestrating events behind the scenes. The dictatorship, economic hardship and natural disasters which devastated Nicaragua are disappearing into the past.

Today Central America has become the "in" place for Americans retiring overseas. The hottest destinations seem to be countries like Nicaragua which were synonymous with strife and civil war. Consequently they were off the beaten path for the majority of tourists, not to mention retirees and much less investors. Now all of this has changed.

A 1998 U.S. News and World Report article touted Nicaragua as a hot new retirement destination, with Central America's lowest crime rate.

At present, Nicaragua can perhaps be most seriously considered the land of opportunity of all the countries in Central America. The country is ripe for investment because it is so underdeveloped. The government, in partiuclar the Nicaraguan Tourism Institute, is bending over backwards to lure investors with the most agessive incentive-filled law in Latin America. They realize the importance of the country's 300 days of sunshine per year and tourist attractions like the country's wide, unspoiled Pacific beaches, wildlife, lakes rivers and volcanoes which are virtually untapped. They know what a potential impact tourism can give the country's economy and have witnessed what the touism boom has meant for neighboring Costa Rica.

As a result of this ambitious effort to boost the tourist trade and other prudent financial polices, foreign investment has jumped from zero to more than 100 million dollars in recent years. A decade of political stability and an improving economic picture have combined to lay the cornerstone for a promising future for the country. Nicaragua has a long way to go, but there appears to be some light at the end of the tunnel with the country on the threshold of an increasing influx of tourists.

Businessmen will be pleased to know the country offers a large under-employed labor pool from which to draw workers. A newly enacted labor code was designed to improve the conditions of workers. The only real drawback is that much of the country's labor is unskilled and will require training.

Nicaragua has a myriad of business opportunities, perfect for the small and medium-sized entrepreneur looking to start a business on a shoestring. You can run a web-based global business by using the Internet, fax machines and cell phones. At present there are over 10,000 people with Internet accounts in Nicaragua.

In general Latin America is a good place to invest. The region has received more foreign investment than any other region in the world — even surpassing Asia. Latin America is also a good place to do business. The opportunities are sizeable and the commercial climate has dramatically improved over the last decade.

With the new millennium upon us, a shrinking world due to better communication, and a burgeoning global economy the possibilities are unlimited for doing business in Central and South America. Trade pacts between Nicaragua, U.S., Mexico and South America will be reality by 2005. They promise to link all of the nations in the hemisphere in to one trading block.

Tax incentives and a government that encourages investments and affords investors virtually the same rights as citizens, contribute to Nicaragua's propitious business climate. Many countries do not permit noncitizens to own property or place restrictions on foreign-owned real estate, but this is not the case in Nicaragua.

You can even purchase your own "piece of paradise" for a fraction of the cost you might pay in the U.S., Canada or even Costa Rica. One gentleman we know of bought a beachfront lot for a mere $20,000 and spent another $30,000 in constructing his dream home. The same home would have cost three times as much in Costa Rica and probably six to ten times as much in California.

People just scaping by on on a small pension or living below the poverty line in the U.S., will be able to live in moderate luxury and upgrade their lifestyle in Nicaragua. Whether you are a retiree or entrepreneur, you'll definately get more "bang for your buck" in Nicaragua.

The government has gone to great lenghts to offer retirees a one-time duty-free exemption. Basically, retirees are only required to have a fixed income of at least four hundred dollars monthly from a pension or annuity. In addition, they are allowed to bring $10,000 worth of their household goods and other personal items duty-free and untaxed when they first arive. Another perk is an exemption from income taxes on income generated from abroad.

The country is not just for retirees, but for those people wanting to retire from their present situations, including burnt-out baby boomers, those tired of dead-end jobs or the rat race. Creative individuals, anyone yearning to pursue their dreams and achieve greater personal growth, and adventurous individuals wanting a more simplified laid-back life style will find Nicaragua a friendly place.

Nicaragua seems fits the bill for people of all ages looking for a an alternative way of life in an exotic land outside of the United States and Canada.

As an expatriate, you have the challenge of immersing yourself in a new culture and even reap the rewards of learning a foreign language. You'll be surprised to know that as an expat you'll make friends easily because foreigners gravitate towards one another.

The country, however, is not for the faint-hearted, but for adventurous souls in search of new horizons and a change of pace. Only these people will reap the rewards of living in a country like Nicaragua. Much like the pioneers who shaped the U.S. in the 19th century, Nicaragua is the "New Frontier.'

THINGS TO THINK ABOUT BEFORE MOVING TO A NEW COUNTRY OR MAKING FOREIGN INVESTMENTS.

- ❏ What is required to become a legal resident? Can I meet these requirements? What is the cost? How often does residency have to be renewed, what are the conditions of renewal and what is the cost?
- ❏ What is required to visit, or stay while you are waiting for residency?
- ❏ What is the political situation? How stable is the country?
- ❏ Weather (Do you like the weather year-round?)
- ❏ Income taxes (Are you taxed on income brought into the country?) (Are you allowed to earn income in the country?) If yes, How is it taxed?
- ❏ Other taxes? (Sales tax, import duties, exit taxes, vehicle taxes, etc.)
- ❏ How much will it cost in fees, duties, and import taxes to bring your personal possessions into the country? (Cars, boats, appliances, electronic equipment, etc.)
- ❏ Rental property - How much? Availability?
- ❏ Purchase property - Property taxes, restrictions on foreign ownership of property, expropriation laws, building regulations, squatters rights, etc. Is there a capital gains tax?
- ❏ Communications - Are there reliable phone and fax lines, cellular phones, beepers, connections to Internet and other computer communication service? Is there good mail service between the country and the rest of the world? Are there private express mail services like DHL, UPS and FEDEX? Are there local newspapers, radio and TV in a language you understand? Is there cable or satellite TV available?
- ❏ Transportation - How are the roads? Are flights available to places you want to go? How are the buses and taxis ? How costly is it to travel to and from other international destinations?
- ❏ Is it difficult for friends and family to visit you?
- ❏ Shopping - Are replacement parts available for the items you have brought from home? If so, what are the costs? If not, how much will it cost to import what you need?
- ❏ Are the types of food you are accustomed to readily available in both markets and restaurants?
- ❏ If you have hobbies, are clubs, supplies and assistance available?
- ❏ What cultural activities are available? (Art, music, theatre, museums, etc.)

- What entertainment is available? (Sports, movies, night clubs, dancing, etc.)
- What recreational facilities are available? (Golf courses, tennis, health clubs, recreational centers, parks, etc.)
- If you like the beach, are good beaches available? Can they be reached easily? What is the year round temperature of the water?
- What is the violent crime rate? Minor crime (theft, car and house break-ins)? What support can be expected from the police department? Are the police helpful to foreign residents?
- How do local residents treat foreign visitors and residents?
- What are the local investment opportunities? Is there any consumer or protective legislation for investors? What return can you expect from your investments? Is the local help reliable? What regulations are involved in hiring employees? What are the employers' responsibilities to the workers?
- Is the banking system safe and reliable? Can they transfer funds and convert foreign currency, checks, drafts, and transfers? Are checking, savings and other accounts available to foreigners? Is there banking confidentiality? Is there a favorable rate of exchange with the U.S. dollar?
- Are good lawyers, accountants, investment advisors and other professionals available?
- How difficult is it to start a business? What kind of opportunities are there?
- How is the health care system? Is it affordable? Do they honor U.S. and Canadian health insurance? Are there any diseases which are dangerous to foreigners, and if so does the local health care system address the problem? What is the quality of hospitals, clinics, doctors and dentists? What is the availability of good specialists?
- How is the sanitation? Can you drink the water? Do the restaurants have good sanitation standards? Are pasteurized milk and other dairy products available? Do meat, fish, and vegetable markets have satisfactory sanitary standards?
- If you are interested in domestic staff, what is the cost of cooks, housekeepers and gardeners, etc.?
- What legislation is there to protect foreign residents? What rights do foreign residents have in comparison to citizens?
- What natural disasters are there? (Hurricanes, tornadoes, typhoons, earthquakes, droughts, floods.)
- Can pets be brought into the country?
- Is there religous freedom?

*Courtesy of the Costa Rican Residents Association

NICARAGUA'S LAND, HISTORY AND PEOPLE

The Lay of the Land

Nicaragua is the largest country in Central America and occupies about the same amount of land as England. It is located in the heart of the Central American isthmus between the Caribbean Sea on the east and on the west by the Pacific Ocean. Nicaragua is bordered by Honduras to the north Costa Rica to the south.

With 54,054 square miles, Nicaragua is divided into three very distinct geographical regions: the Pacific lowlands, the north-central mountains, and the Caribbean lowlands also called the Mosquito Coast or Mosquitia. The Pacific lowlands are interrupted by about 40 volcanoes (the country has a total of 58) of which San Cristóbal and Concepción are the largest and most imposing.

The country's most prominent feature is Lake Nicaragua, the largest lake in Central America and the 10th largest freshwater lake in the world with a surface area of about 8,157 sq. km. The lake is also famous because in it live the world's only fresh water sharks. Scientists think the lake was originally connected to the sea and was cut off by an earthquake or

NICARAGUA GENERAL INFORMATION

Capital	Managua
Population	4,275,000 (growth rate 3.4%),
Size	50,054 square miles
Quality of Life	Excellent,(friendly people, affordable)
Official Language	Spanish (Creole English spoken in some areas)
Political System	Democractic Republic
Currency	Córdoba
Investment Climate	Excellent-many opportunities
Official Religion	Roman Catholic 95% Protestant 5%
People	69% mestizo, 17% European descent, 9% African descent, 5% indigenous peoples
Foreign Population	Over 5,000 (U.S.)
Longevity	64 years male, 69 years female
Literacy	65.7%
Time	Central Standard (U.S.)

NICARAGUA'S LAND, HISTORY AND PEOPLE

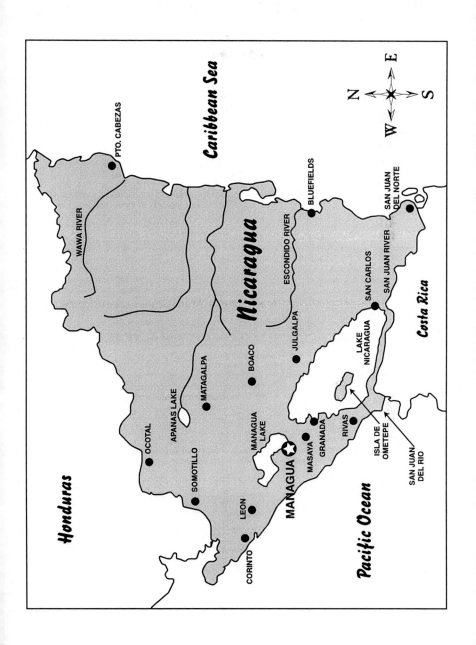

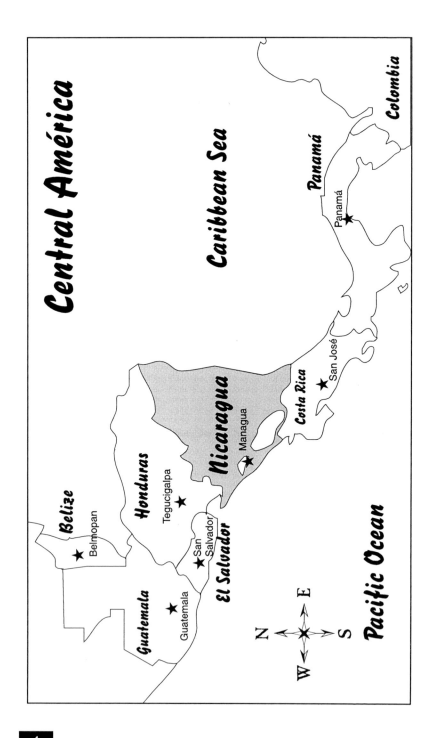

NICARAGUA'S LAND, HISTORY AND PEOPLE

changes in the land formation.

Lake Managua is the country's other important lake. There are several smaller volcanic lakes near or right inside the city limits of Managua. Laguna Masaya and La Laguna de Apoyo are interesting lakes which lie in volcanic basins.

Weather

Like other areas in Central AmericaNicaragua's climate varies according to altitude with different regions of the country having distinct climates.

The Pacific lowands are always extremely hot. The Pacific dry season or summer becomes very dusty, especially when the wind begins to below in February. The mountainous region in the north is much cooler than the lowlands. The Caribbean part of the country is hot and wet, and rain can fall heavily even in the "dry" season.

As in most tropical regions, Nicaragua has a dry season (*la estación seca*) or summer from November to May and a rainy season (*invierno*) which roughly runs from May to October. Nicaragua can be called the land of eternal summer in that there is not much difference in temperature from month to month and from season to season. In general, average temperatures range between 80 to 90 degrees F during the dry season and between 85 to 95 degrees F in the rainy season. The lowest average temperature is 77 degrees F and the highest is 104 degrees F. Managua and Pacific part of Nicaragua are usually far less rainy than most of Central America.

Where to Live in Nicaragua

Since we have just discussed Nicaragua's geography and weather, now is a good time to talk about some of the things to consider before choosing a permanent place to live.

Deciding where to live in Nicaragua depends on your preferences. If you like the stimulation of urban living you will probably be happiest living in **Managua**, **León** or **Granada**. Living in a foreign country represents a big change for many people because they often find themselves with more free time than usual and sometimes get bored. As we mention later in this book, there are sufficient activities to keep everyone busy and happy in Nicaragua. You are more likely to find more to do around larger cities and towns than in rural areas. However, laid back types can find it easy to get away from it all by living in the countryside or at the beach.

Managua is the country's largest city and is spread across the southern shore of Lake Managua. It is also country's capital and main commmercial center. The city is crowded with more than a million people — a quarter of the country's population.

A number of natural disasters have devastated the city and left parts in shambles. The colonial city was destroyed by an earthquake in 1931. It was rebuilt only to be destroyed by another earthquake in 1972. After the 1972 earthquake, the city's center was not rebuilt. Thus the city has no real downtown. Much of what was formerly the center of the city has been decentralized with shopping centers, markets and residential areas now located on the outskirts of the city.

Like most cities in Nicaragua, Managua has few street names, although some important streets are named. People get around by using landmarks and cardinal points. Locations will be given in relation to famous landmarks. To compound matters, locations are sometimes given in relation to where landmarks used to be before they were destroyed by the 1972 earthquake. A typical direction might be given like this: "From the corner store two blocks north and one block south."

The city has its share of banks, a post office, hotels for all

NICARAGUA'S LAND, HISTORY AND PEOPLE

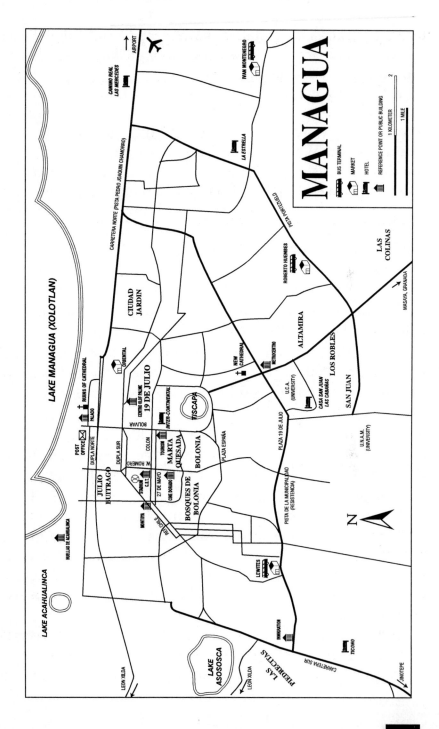

budgets, first-class restaurants, hospitals and other basic services. There are also universities, foreign language schools, museums, baseball games, a large central market, and much more. The city is currently undergoing a building boom and many locals are beginning to refer to the the city as "The New Managua." A number of new luxury hotels, like the Intercontinental, have been built with more on the way. International cusine as well as fast food chains like McDonalds, Subway, Pizza Hut, Domino's Pizza and Burger King are found all over the city. There are couple of new shoping centers including the mammoth **Metro Center Mall** which rivals any U.S. shopping center. Numerous upscale stores, a CineMark movie theater from the U.S. and food court can be found at this state-of-the-art mall.

The country's international airport, Augusto Cesar Sandino is located about 8 miles from the city.

One of the best things about Managua is that many of the country's best attractions are conveniently located nearby, making the capital a good home base from which you may explore the country.

Managua is not our first choice for living because of its hot climate, but as you can see from the above, there are adequate infrastructure and plenty to do to keep busy and happy.

One of the potentially best places to reside is **Granada** — the country's third-largest city after Managua and León. Located on the shores of lake Managua, Granada is without a doubt the country's most colorful city and has a cozy, laid-back ambiance. This charming colonial city is tourist friendly and, therefore, has become one of the country's main tourist attractions.

A long-time expat who lives in Granada boldly boasted, "Granada is not Nicaragua nor Latin America. It is the way Latin America used to be 100 years ago. Granada is the oldest

NICARAGUA'S LAND, HISTORY AND PEOPLE

and culturally richest city in Latin America. Among the people there is a type of old family unity not found in other places in the modern world. The place seems to be caught in a time warp."

With a population of only 75,000, Granada has managed to maintain its historic atmosphere and feel of a small town. The city is so quaint you can even travel around the city in a horse-drawn carriage. Foreigners have realized this; there is a growing expatriate community taking root. In fact, a new American Legion Post is currently being organized with expats welcome to join.

A number of foreigners who reside permanently there and others who visit quite frequently from Costa Rica.

One of the salient features of the city is its strong colonial character. The churches and homes of the city have conserved their original colonial flavor. Spanish-style homes with beautiful

Colonial-style houses give Granada its charm.

NICARAGUA'S LAND, HISTORY AND PEOPLE

interior courtyards abound.

We know of a couple of Americans who are restoring some of these beautiful homes. One plans to covert his home into a small hotel for his travel business.

Granada has its share of supermarkets, a couple of places to see movies, banks, a post office, an affordable country club and a basic infrastructure. Believe it or not there isn't a traffic light in town.

Some of the city's interesting sites are Casa del Tres Mundos, Iglesia Convent of San Francisco, La Polvera, the Cementerio and a train station located in a beautiful, Neo-Classic building.

Despite being a small city Granada has its share of cultural events including the annual Latin American Film Festival and Book Fair.

Hospedaje Central, La Fábrica, Las Alemanes and **Charly's Bar** are local hangouts where you can savor a Victoria, the local

Horse-drawn carriages are still used to get around Granada.

beer, and find some expats and locals with whom to talk.

Since the city attracts people from all over the world you can expect to meet a variety of interesting people. A definite bohemian atmosphere pervades the city. Stop by the Hospedaje Central and talk with the colorful owner, Bill. He'll fill your ears full of information about the local scene.

Every Friday night, an entertaining festival is held in Parque Colón, the main plaza. It is the most important cultural event of the week. Cesar's is a popular disco found in the Centro Turístico next to the lake. The place really rocks on the weekends.

The city also offers a beachfront park where you can swim in the lake. You can tour the off-shore islands (Las Isletas) which are found in the area. The nearby **Mirador de Catarina** is a memorable spot situated on the top of a volcano overlooking the **Laguna de Apoyo**. The pristine volcanic crater is filled with water (sort of a mini-Lake Tahoe). Beyond the lake you can see the city of Granada in the distance. It is truly a sight to behold.

There is e-mail and Internet service available at **Computadoras de Granada** (552-3368) where you can keep in touch with the outside world and and can arrange to have an Internet line installed in your home or business.

Masaya (population.100,000) is located 11 miles west of Granada. Known as "the city of the flowers," the city is located on the edge of a crater lake, Laguna Masaya. On the opposite side looms the Masaya Volcano with a plume of steam spewing out of its crater. It is the most visited of all the country's volcanos, having become popular with tourists in recent years. Adventuous souls can even reach the crater and get a first-hand glimpse of volcanic activity. The volcano's many lookout points also afford spectacular views of the surrounding countryside. On a clear day you can see all the way to Lake Managua

www.primenicaraguaproperty.com

"Make your dreams come true by purchasing a home or land in beautiful Nicaragua at affordable prices."

Many saavy investors consider Nicaragua to be the **LAND OF OPPORTUNITY** and the last true **FRONTIER**. Now is your **CHANCE** to get in on the ground floor of the Nicaraguan **LAND RUSH** by owning a piece of **PARADISE**. Few **OPPORTUNITIES** exisit anywhere in the world like you'll find in Nicaragua.

Here is what's available:

* **Perkoff Realty** is offering **PREMIER** properities in colonial **GRANADA**, Nicaragua. Granada is one of the few cities in Latin America which retains its colonial charm and flavor. The whole city is a living monument to Nicaragua's colonial past. The architecture is truly impressive. Beautiful colonial comes with large interior courtyards abound. All this set against a backdrop of towering volcanos and Lake Nicaragua. The city has a very laid-back tranquil atmosphere.

***REMAX Realty** of Granada has a ample selection of homes and land from which to choose.

***Beachfront** properties are also **PLENTIFUL** at "rock bottom" prices at San Juan del Sur and other areas. See: **www.nicaraguanland.com**

Just tell us what you want and we'll contact you:
buynicaragua@hotmail.com
or Fax: 011-506-261-8968

NICARAGUA'S LAND, HISTORY AND PEOPLE

Managua and Granada. The city boasts two large markets where local artists sell their wares.

León is Nicaragua's second largest city. It is on the shore of Lake Managua. León was founded the same year as Granada, in 1524 by Francisco Hernández de Córdoba and is one of the country's oldest cities. It was the capital of Nicaragua throughout the colonial period, until Managua became the capital in 1857. León is traditionally the most liberal of Nicaragu'a cities and remains the radical and intellectual center of the country.

The city continues to maintain the grandeur and splendor of the colonial period. Its narrow paved streets, adobe homes with their gardens, red-tiled roofs and weathered buildings have made the city's architecture its main attraction. Gorgeous traditional country homes can be found in neighborhoods like San Felipe. Monuments to the revolution, including some Sandinista murals, abound. León is the home of the largest cathedral in Central America. In recent years there has been a lot of restoration going on. Restaurants, a post office and other basic services are found in the city.

Despite its rich historical past, León is primarily known as a center for artesanía or handicrafts. The best place to see handicrafts is at the Mercado de Artesanías or Artisans' Market. Since the city is also famous for music and festivals together with its handicrafts, it is sometimes referred to as the "Folklore Capital" of Nicaragua. One "can't-miss" attraction is the **Museo Rubén Dario**, the house where the country's most famous poet spent his childhood.

Outside theLeón, one can find other interesting attractions. As you will see in this section there are a couple of warm, surprisingly uncrowded beaches within an hour's drive from the city. Nearby rivers also offer a place to relax and pass the time fishing.

For those of you who don't like hot weather, the city of **Matagalpa** might just be the place you are looking for. The town is located in a verdant mountain valley with a river beside it. The climate is cool and refreshing compared to the warm lowlands. Many foreigners say that the climate is similar to the spring-like weather found in some parts of Costa Rica's Central valley. This area is really beautiful and an abundance of fauna and flora make it a great place to walk or hike.

Estelí is another nice town in the montains. There is a lot of tobacco grown in this area. Some of the best cigars in the world are said the come from there.

Nicaragua is often referred to as the "land of water" because its landscape is dominated by its lakes, rivers and beaches. Without a doubt the country's lakes and beaches are definitetly reason for considering moving to Nicaragua.

One foreigner we interviewed, who plans to move to Granada, says he can't wait to buy himself a boat so he can explore the lake and its islands. Another expat we talked to has built his dream home on the Pacific coast so he can partake

A view of Lake Nicaragua from Granada.

NICARAGUA'S LAND, HISTORY AND PEOPLE

in watersports.

Speaking of the Pacific coast, there are several beaches about an hour's drive from Managua. **Pochomil** is a clean swimming beach with a few hotels and bars in the area. Because of its proximity to Managau it is very popular with Nicaraguans. **Masachapa** to the north is not as nice as Pochomil. It tends to be a little run down for foreigners' tastes.

About three miles up the coast from Pochomil is **Montelimar**. It used to be the famous beach house and summer retreat of the dictator Somoza. When the Sandinistas took power they turned Montelimar into a resort. Recently it was refurbished by the Spanish hotel chain Barceló. Despite being upscale the resort is surprising affordable by international standards.

To the north, about 30 miles south of the city of León, are two beaches worth exploring. **El Velero** is a decent beach with water which is ideal for surfing and swimming. **El Tránsito** is another beach to visit. Moving south are **La Boquita** and **Cesares**, **Huehuete**, **Veracruz** and **El Astillero** It is difficult to get to some of these beaches because of either their remote location or the condition of the roads. **Salinas Grande** and **Jiquilillo** are good beaches.

Located in a large curved bay, **San Juan del Sur** is considered a leading beach resort. The town has hotels, good seafood, sportfishing and surfing. Check out both **Marie's Bar** and **Restaurant.** and **Richard's Bar** and **Restaurant**. **Hotel Casa Blanca** (505) 045-82135 is a clean place to stay right on the main drag. A small number of foreigners live in this seaside port on a permanent basis.

It must be pointed out that residing at the beach can grow old after a while. There is not a whole lot to do and little infrastructure. Beach combers, sun worshipers, surfers and fishermen, however, will feel right at home in a beach area.

If the beach isn't to your liking there are always the lakes. **Isla Ometepe** is an imposing beauty. It is purported to be the largest fresh water island in the world and sits roughly in the center of the Lake Nicaragua. This spectacular island is of volcanic origin and its two volcanos, **Volcán Concepción** and **Volcán Madera** dominate the panorama. Concepción is considered to be a perfect cone and rises to a height of 1610 meters from the lake. Volcán Madera is smaller at 1310 meters high.

The lakes warm clear water, gentle sandy slopes and small waves make for optimum swimming conditions. A rain forest, an abundance of wildlife, including several types of monkeys, parrots, iguanas and many kinds of birds, are found on the island.

The island doesn't offer 'big-city' type of attractions but is suitable for walking or exploring on horseback. There are severla hotels and restaurants on the island. Ometepe is really for those types of people who are tired of the urban hustle and bustle and want to get away from it all. Life here is so slow that during the turbulent 1970's and 1980's life on the island remained virtually unaffected by events which transpired on the mainland.

We have not included all of areas of the country, but only those which we feel offer the most potential to expats. We suggest that before choosing a place to live that you explore the country and read all of the books we have listed in Chapter 10 of this book in the section titled, "Suggested Reading.'

A Great One-of-a-Kind Tour

One way to see Nicaragua which we highly recommend is to take one of the introductory tours operated by either **Travel Net** or **Live in Nicaragua Tours**. Both tour companies

NICARAGUA'S LAND, HISTORY AND PEOPLE

provided exciting fact-filled tours.
   Below is a sample itineray from a recent tour.

Day 1 :
Arrival
Ground transportation from the airport to the hotel in downtown Managua.

Day 2 :
Breakfast at the hotel
Morning bus trip around Managua (markets, malls, hospital, schools, neighborhoods where you might want to live etc.)
Lunch Break
<u>Afternoon Seminar</u>
Topics:
   a) Residency
   b) Other Services
   c) Health care options
   d) Real Estate
   e) Moving to Nicaragua
   f) Banking
Dinner

Day 3 :
Breakfast at the hotel
Bus trip to Montelimar Beach Resort. Lunch at the Hotel. Afternoon for recreation. Dinner at the hotel.

Day 4 :
Breakfast at the hotel, followed by a trip by bus to the charming colonial city of Granada. Lunch, followed by a city tour in the afternoon. Dinner with local real estate people.

Day 5 :
Breakfast at the hotel
Trip to Isletas near Granada. Afternoon trip to La Laguna de

Apoyo. Stop along the way to look for handicrafts. Free Night.
Day 6 :
Option A: Breakfast at the hotel. Trip to the Masaya volcano. Market tour of Masaya and lunch at Aiport 79.

Option B: Day trip to Ometepec Island from San Jorge.

Day 7:
Breakfast at the hotel
Depart for Managua with transportation provided.

*The above itinerary is subject to change.

All trips are led by Christopher Howard the author of this guidebook and expert on living and investing in Central America. For additional information contact: **Central America.com** Toll-free: 800-493-8426 or E-mail tico@gate.net, or visit www.ticotravel.com. **Live in Nicaragua** is another tour company. Contact them Toll-free at: 619-461-6131 , E-mail crbooks@racsa.co.cr. or see www.liveinnicaragua.com.

Nicaragua's History in Brief

The earliest vestiges of humans in Nicaragua date from about 10,000 years ago. During the pre-Colombian period the Nicaraos, Chortegas, Chontales and Miskitos were some of the native inhabitants of the country. Indigenous people from Mexico immigrated to the country's Pacific lowlands. Eventually the Aztec culture was adopted by many indigenous groups when the Aztecs moved south during the 15th century to establish a trading colony.

The first contact with Europeans was in 1502 when Columbus sailed down the Caribbean coast. In 1524, with the

NICARAGUA'S LAND, HISTORY AND PEOPLE

arrival of Francisco Hernández de Córdoba, the first two cities, Granada first and then León, were founded. Eventually Nicaragua moved its capital from Granada to León and finally to Managua in 1858.

In 1821 Nicaragua as well as the rest of Central America, was freed from Spanish rule. Complete independence was finally obtained by 1838. Shortly after that, Britain and the U.S. became attracted to Nicarauga in search of a shortcut across the Isthmus via the Río San Juan and Lake Nicaragua.

In 1855 the infamous American, William Walker, appeared on the scene and his saga began. Walker, with his band of rag-tag mercenaries, attempted to take over Nicaragua. He proclaimed himself president, but was eventually driven from the country and executed in Honduras in 1860.

Different personalities governed the country afterwards. Among them was the dictator José Santos Zelaya. He refused to give the U.S the exclusive right to build a canal from the Pacific to the Atlantic. Consequently, the U.S. signed a canal treaty with Panama. Due to political instability, Nicaragua remained under U.S. occupation for the first half of the 20th century. In 1934, General Anastasio "Tacho" Somoza, head of the country's U.S.-trained National Guard, had the liberal oppostion leader, Agusto Sandino shot. After fraudulent elections Somoza became president in 1937.

Somoza ruled Nicaragua as a dictator for the next 20 years, amassing a personal fortune and land holdings the size of El Salvador. Together with his family he virtually owned the whole country. His personal fortune was estimated to be around 50 million dollars by the mid-fifties. General Somoza was assasinated in 1956. His two sons each served a presidential term and the youger, General Anastasio Somoza Debayle, dominated the country from 1963 until he was forced from power in 1979. He was later assasinated in Paraguay.

In 1972 Nicaragua was devastated by an earthquake. Unfortunately, international aid went straight into the pockets of Somoza while thousands of people suffered. As a result, oppositon to Somoza's rule spread to all classes of Nicaraguans. Soon a general revolt united moderates and the more radical FSLN (*Frente Sandinista de Liberacion Nacional*) to oust Somoza on July 19, 1979.

The government headed by the Sandinistas quietly nationalized the Somozas' large land holdings and established farming cooperatives. They reduced illiteracy from 50% to 13% and instituted widespread health care.

Fear spread of Soviet influence through Central America. The U.S. then tried to destablize the Sandinista government because of its left-wing tendencies. Aid was suspended to Nicaragua and 10 million dollars were allocated for organizing counter revolutionary group known as *contras*. In 1985 the U.S. even imposed a five-year trade embargo in an effort to rid Nicaragua of the Sandinistas. What this essentially did was to destroy the Nicaraguan economy.

Nicaraguans, unhappy with the Sandinistas unfullfilled promises for an improved economy and peace, voted against them in the 1990 elections and elected Violeta Chamorro president. However, she proved ineffective as president and failed to revive the economy. So, in 1997 Arnoldo Alemán was elected president.

Peace and stability have been the country's main accomplishments in the 1990's. In an effort to improve the economy and promote private enterprise, many of the country's state-run corporations have been privatized. The government has also tried to promote tourism and foreign investment with a whole slew of attractive incentives. Unfortunately, the majority of Nicaraguans have not yet reaped the economic benefits causing thousands of Nicaraguans to emigrate to Costa Rica in search of work.

If political stability and foreign aid and investment continue

NICARAGUA'S LAND, HISTORY AND PEOPLE

the country is bound to move forward.

Government

The Nicaraguan government is a constitutional democracy with executive, legislative, judicial branches of government. Executive power is vested in the president, who is assisted by a vice president and an appointed cabinet. The president's term is six years. The legislative branch is made up of a unicameral 93-member National (constituent) Assembly, directly elected to a six-year term, by popular vote on a propotional representation basis.

Nicaragua is divided into 16 departamentos (Departments or provinces) in two zones, and one special one. The Pacific Zone consists of: Nueva Segovia, Madriz, Estelí, León, Chinandega, Managua, Masaya, Granada, Carazo, Rivas, Boaco, Chontales, Matagalpa and Jinotega. The Atlantic Zone: Atlantic North Autonomuos Region, Atlantic South Autononmous Region, and Río San Juan special zone.

Nicaragua has had 11 constitutions. The new constitution provides for freedom of speech and press, peaceful assembly, freedom of assembly, freedom of religion and movement within the country, as well as foreign travel, emigration and repatriation.

Under the Chamorro government the size of the army was reduced from 80,000 to 15,000 and the military draft was ended. Attempts are being made to reduce the military's power by placing it under civilian control.

Economy

Traditionally Nicaraguahas always been an agriculture-based economy. Coffee has been the most important crop.

Bananas, sugar cane, rice and tobacco have also contributed to the economy.

As of 1999 the grwoth of the country's gross domestic product (GDP) was 6.3%; per capita income was around $450; and inflation was around 11%.

Nicaragua's present and past economic woes can best be summed-up by a Nicaraguan citizen who related to us in Spanish, "*Nicaragua es un país salado*" (Nicaragua is an unlucky country). The word '*salado*' means unlucky or cursed. A combination of natual catastrophes, external events and the legacy of the Somozas have impeded the country's economic progress. The Somoza family turned the country into their personal fiefdom. It is estimated the family controlled 'a lion's share' of the country's import and export businesses, a national airline, a construction business, a huge portion of the country's arable land and much more. On top of that Somoza further enriched himself by taking the relief monies after the 1972 earthquake as we alluded to earlier.

The Sandinistas tried to improve the economy but fell short because of the embargo by the U.S. and the war against the contras which ate up all of their budget. However there were some surprising economic gains during the first years of their regime. On top of all this huricane Juana forced the government spend huge sums of money on emergency aid. The Chomorro government tried to stimulate private enterprise, but came up short. Alemán has tried to improve the economy but has been plagued by a corruption scandle. As of May 2000 unemployment is still very high.

To make matters worse, in November 1998 huricane Mitch caused massive destruction along the Atlantic coast of Central America. The hurricane, a class 5, caused mudslides, washed out bridges and roads and killed thousands of people. In Nicaragua heavy rains in the wake of the storm caused a huge mudslide that burried several villages. Thousands of people were left homeless or died as a result of the hurricane, one of the strongest recorded this century.

At present, foreign investment, private enterprise and a growing tourism market seem to be the keys to improving the economy. Since the Sandinista era the democratically elected governments have made significant progress in attracting foreign investment. An incentived-packed Foreign Investment law which includes a tourism section is bound to help the country in the long run. Tourism became Nicaragua's third most important source of foreign exchange by 1998 and is expected to grow by 25%, to around a half million visitors, by the year 2002. Major hotel chains like Holiday Inn and Barceló have taken advantage of Nicaragua's new tax law providing tax breaks for the hospitality and lodging industry.

The country is ripe for foreign investment beacuse it is so underdeveloped. It abounds with opportunities for creative entrepreneurs.

The People

Besides its excellent weather and natural beauty, Nicaragua's warm-hearted hard-working people are probably the country's most important resource and one of the main factors to consider in selecting Nicaragua as a place to live, retire or invest. The country's friendly and humble people will go out of their way to make foreigners feel at home.

Nicaraguans proudly call themselves *nicas*. About 77% of the country's people are mestizo, a mixture of Spanish and Indian ancestry, make up the majority of the population. Other ethnic goups include Spanish and other Europeans 10%; blacks 9%; Indians 4%. The largest concentration of Indians are the Miskitos who live in the north eastern area.

Nicaragua society is a society of classes. This stratified

society has virtually existed in one form or another since pre colonial times with little social mobility. As in Mexico, the lighter one's skin, the higher one is likely to be on the social scale. People can improve their social status by marrying lighter-skinned people. Those of European ancestry have traditionally made up the upper rungs of society and business.

The country has a population of around 4,200,000 people and this amount is expected to reach 5,000,000 within the year. About 500,000 Nicaraguans have emigrated to Costa rica over the last 15 years in search of work. Until the country's economy improves there is no reason to believe this trend will change.

Family ties are very important in Nicaragua. There is a lot of nepotism with the man ruling the roost. About 95% of the population is Roman Catholic and 5% is Protestant. Freedon of religion does exist.

As far the arts go, Nicaragua is often said to be a nation of poets. Poetry is considered to be one of the country's most important and beloved arts.

Nicaragua's literary tradition dates back to the colonial

Nicaragua's warm-hearted people are a treasure.

NICARAGUA'S LAND, HISTORY AND PEOPLE

era. No other Central American nation comes close to Nicaragua's literary output.

The most well-known literary figure is Rubén Darío (1867-1916). He was know as the "Prince of Spanish American Lierature." His works inspired poetry movements and literary trends through Latin America.

Ceramic arts are part of Nicaragua's artistic traditions and can be found for sale in many markets. Masaya has a market where local artisans exhibit their wares.

Music is an integral part of daily life in Nicaragua. Nicaraguans, like most Latins love salsa, merengue, reggae, Spanish rock and American pop music and don't miss the opportunity to party and dance.. Everywhere you go music fills the air. Like Costa Rica and Guatemala, the national instrument is the marimba. Raeggae music is poplular on the English-speaking Caribbean coast, especially in Bluefields.

Despite all their admirable qualities, there is a negative side to the character of the Nicaraguan people. Nicaraguans suffer from many of the same problems endemic to all Latin American societies. Corruption and bribery are a way of life; bureaucratic ineptitude and red-tape thrive; the concepts of punctuality and logical reasoning are almost non-existent by North American standards, and the "Manaña Syndrome"—of leaving for tomorrow what can be done today—seems to be the norm rather than the exception.

Like most countries in Latin America manliness is well-entrenched.Unfortunately, as in most Latin American countries, *machismo* is prevalent to some degree among Nicaragun males. *Machismo* is the belief in the natural superiority of men in all fields of endeavor. It becomes the obsession and constant preoccupation of many Latin men to demonstrate they are *macho* in a variety of ways. Fortunately, the Nicaraguan version of *machismo* is milder than the type found in Mexico but it nevertheless exists.

There is no telling to what lengths some men will go in order to demonstrate their virility. A man's virility is measured by the number of seductions or *conquistas* he makes. It is not unusual for married men to have a *querida* or lover. Many even have children with their mistresses. Since many married men don't want to risk having a lover, they sleep with prostitutes or loose women called *zorras*. For this reason many Nicaraguan women prefer foreign men to Nicaraguan men.

Foreign women walking along the street will be alarmed by the flirtatious behavior and outrageous comments of some Nicaraguan men. Many of these flirtations or *piropos*, as they are called in Spanish, may border on the obscene but are usually harmless forms of flattery to get a female's attention . Foreign women are wise to ignore this and any other manifestations of Latin men's efforts to prove their *machismo*.

Sadly, many Central Americans have misconceptions about North Americans' wealth. A few people seem to think that all Americans and Canadians are millionaires. It is easy to understand why many *nicas* think this way because of the heavy influence of the U.S. television and movies which depict North Americans as being very affluent. Also, the only contact many Nicaraguan's have with Americans is primarily with tourists, who are usually living high on the hog and spending freely while on vacation.

It is therefore not surprising that some individuals will try to take advantage of foreigners by overcharging them for services and goods. Others will use very persuasive means to borrow amounts of money ranging from pocket change to larger sums of money and have no intention of ever paying the debt. Please, take our advice: don't lend money to anyone, however convincing the sob story.

Some foreigners, who have married Central American

NICARAGUA'S LAND, HISTORY AND PEOPLE

women, have been "taken to the cleaners." Because family ties are so strong and there is much poverty in parts of Central America, you can end up supporting your spouse's whole family. We talked to one retired American in Costa Rica who couldn't live on his two thousand dollar a month pension because he had to support not only his wife and stepchildren, but his wife's sister's children as well. Furthermore, he had to lend his father-in-law money to pay off a second mortgage because the bank was going to repossess the latter's house.

This is an extreme example, but we have heard many similar stories while living in Central America. Not all Nicaraguan families are like this one, but it doesn't hurt to be aware that the situation exists. Be careful with whom you get involved. (See Chapter 5 "Finding Companionship" for more on this subject.)

We suggest that you don't dwell on these negatives and hope you realize how difficult it is to generalize about or stereotype any group of people. After you have resided in Nicaragua and experienced living with the people, you will be able to make your own judgements.

"Seminole Indians Eye Nicaragua for Investments"

A 95-room hotel housing Managua's largest restaurant and dance floor -the Hard Rock Cafe- opens next month, the product of the most unlikely of investors: the Seminole Tribe of Florida.

The 2,500-member tribe, based in Hollywood in South Florida, is pouring big money into Nicaragua's capital, hoping to jump in early on a wave of foreign investment. So far, the tribe has put about $10 million into a hotel and restaurant, in addition to a $3.5 million cattle ranch purchased two years ago.

The tribe picked Managua because the nation long torn by civil war is in the midst of an economic rush, so real estate and labor still come cheap. Nicaragua, plagued with poverty, years of political instability and natural disasters, has recently enjoyed a 5 percent growth in its economy. "Nicaragua will turn around and is turning around," tribe operations officer Tim Cox said. "We're making the bet that Nicaragua will not be the second-poorest country in the hemisphere in a few years. We think it will be one of the wealthiest."

The Seminoles have purchased from Orlando-based Hard Rock the franchise for all of Central and South America and the Caribbean. They expect to break ground in Costa Rica in two months and hope to have six to eight restaurants within 18 months. They're also in negotiations with the Hooters chain and studying whether there is a market for casinos in Nicaragua. The tribe will soon take over the Hard Rock Cafes in Buenos Aires and Lima, Cox said.

The Seminoles' Nicaragua venture -- the 300-seat, 7,200-square-foot Managua Hard Rock -- is scheduled to open in May. The hotel is located near several new corporate offices and its managers plan to target business travelers.

It was originally slated to be a Ramada Inn, but halfway through construction, financing fell through. "The Seminoles intervened," said tourism minister Rene Molina. "It was half-done, and they finished it. The Seminoles have hotels and casinos with tremendous success. We expect the same here."

SAVING MONEY IN NICARAGUA

How Much Does it Cost to Live in Nicaragua?

An important factor that determines the cost of living for foreigners in Nicaragua is their lifestyle. If you are used to a wealthy lifestyle, you'll spend more than someone accustomed to living frugally. But either way, you will still find Nicaragua to be a bargain when compared to Costa Rica, Mexico, and most of the other countries in Latin America.

Your purchasing power is greater in Nicaragua than in the United States or Canada. The country is really less expensive when compared to most places.

Housing costs only a fraction of what it does in the U. S. and hired help is a steal. Utilities—telephone service, electricity, and water— are cheaper than in North America. You never need to heat your home or apartment because of Nicaragua's warm climate. Public transportation is also inexpensive. Bus fares to the provinces cost no more than $6 to the farthest part in the country. Taxi travel is also affordable. For example, to go anywhere in Granada the most you pay is about 40 cents.

A gallon of regular gasoline of gas costs about $2.00 However, you don't really need a car because public transportation is so inexpensive. If you must have a new car, remember that new cars more expensive than in the U.S. due to import duties of about 20-30%. Because of this, people keep their cars for a long time and take good care of them. We recommend buying used cars since they are usually in good mechanical condition and their resale value is excellent. Food, entertainment and, above all, health care, are surprisingly affordable. Both new and second-hand furniture is priced very low.

When you have lived in Nicaragua a while, learned the ins-and- outs and made some friends and contacts, you can cut your living costs more by sharing a house or apartment, house-sitting in exchange for free rent, working full or part-time (if you can find legal work), starting a small business or bartering within the expatriate community, doing without packaged and canned imported brand-name foods and buying local products, eating in small cafes instead of expensive restaurants, or buying fresh foods in bulk at the Central Market like Nicaraguans do. You can also help yourself by learning Spanish so you can bargain and get lower prices when shopping.

If you take lessons from the locals and live a modest lifestyle, you can save a lot of money and still enjoy yourself. By not following a U.S.-"shop-till-you-drop" mentality you can live reasonably.

Taking all of the aforementioned and personal lifestyles into consideration, the minimum needed for a decent standard of living for a single person ranges from $500-$600 monthly. You can indeed live for as little as $20 a day in cluding housing. We know one retiree who lives comfortably in Granada for $500 per month including a full-time maid. Some single people scrape by on considerably less and others spend hundreds of dollars more, again depending on the lifestyle to which one is accustomed.

SAVING MONEY IN NICARAGUA

A couple can live well on $1,000 per month, and live in luxury for $1,500. Couples with husband and wife both receiving good pensions can live even better. Remember, two in Nicaragua can often live as cheaply as one. Any way you look at it, you will enjoy a higher standard of living in Nicargua and get more for your money. Consider that the average Nicaraguan earns less than $100 a month.

Approximate Cost of Living and Prices as of October 2000 in U.S. Dollars*

Rentals - Monthly
House (small, unfurnished) $160
House (large, luxurious) $500
Apartment (small, 1–2 bedrooms, unfurnished).......$250+
Apartment (large, luxurious) ....$500+
Property Taxes................................Almost nothing

Home Prices
House (small)...$35,000+
House (large) ....$80,000+

Miscellaneous..**Monthly**
Electric Bill (apt.) $15
Water-Sewage (apt.) $5
Telephone (calls within the country)....................$10
Cable TV $12
Direct TV..$30
Taxi........................about 25 cents for a short distance
Bus Fares (around city).....................................$.15
Gasoline (regular gas).........................$2.00 per gallon
Maid/Gardener (full time)....................$60 per month
Restaurant Meal (inexpensive) ....$5.00+
Soda (a diner or coffee shop) Meal....................$2.00

Restaurant (mid-range)	$10.00
Banana (dozen)	$.60
Soft drink	$.65
Pineapple	$.33
Papaya	$.75
Lettuce	$.20
Cereal (large box of corn flakes)	$1.50
Bread (loaf)	$.75
Tuna (small can)	$1.25
Orange	$.08
Rice (1lb.)	$1.40
Steak(lb).	$1.90
Quart of Milk	$.95
Beer	$.45
Beans (5 lbs.)	$1.50
Airmail Letter	around $.33 to the U.S.
Doctor's Visit	$10-25
New Automobile	U.S. prices plus around 30% duty
Used Car	U.S. prices plus around 30% duty

* These prices are subject to fluctuations.

Tipping

The majority of Nicaraguans don't leave tips in inexpensive restaurants. In upscale restaurants you may leave up to 10% of the bill which is usually included in the bill.. There are some restaurants which include a service charge with the bill. Of course, employees such as bellhops and taxi drivers are appreciative of any additional gratuity for excellent service. Since the cost of living and prices are so reasonable in Nicaragua the amount of most tips will be relatively low.

Affordable Hired Help

As you know, full or part-time domestic help, is hard to find and prohibitively expensive for the average person, not to mention a retiree, in the United States. This is not the case in Nicaragua. The country has the lowest minimum wage of $62.66 per month of any of the Central American countries. A live-in maid or other full-time help usually costs $50 to $60 per month. Agriculture and sanitary workers make $35.47, a chauffer $42.20 and a contruction worker make $94.59 repectively per month. Often you can hire a couple for a bargain price with the woman working as a maid and the man working as a full-time gardener and watchman.

In Nicaragua a maid can do everything from washing clothes to taking care of small children. You can also use your maid to stand in line for you or run errands and bargain for you in stores, since foreigners often pay more for some items because of their naivety and poor language skills.

Foreigners can hire a full-time maid for around $65 a month

General handymen and carpenters are also inexpensive. If you are infirm, one of the above people can assist you with many daily tasks. To find quality help, check with other expats for references or ask around.

Conditions of work are covered by several labor laws and are also spelled out by article 1987 of the Nicaraguan constitution. The constitution specifies no more than an eight-hour workday in a forty-eight-hour work week, with an hour of rest each day. Health and safety standards are also provided for by the constitution and forced labor is prohibited.

The Labor Code of 1945, patterened after Mexican labor laws, was Nicaragua's first major labor legislation. Provisions of the code prohibited more than three hours overtime, three times a week. Workers were entitled to fifteen days of vacation annually (eight national holidays and seven saint's days).

The Nicaraguan social security program, passed in 1957, enumerates workers' benefits, including maternity, medical, death, and survivors' benefits; pensions and workers' compensation for disability.

The constitution provides for the right to bargain collectively. In addition, the Labor Code 1945 was amended in 1962 to allow for sympathy strikes, time off with pay when a worker has been given notice of an impending layoff, and the right to claim unused vacation pay when terminated. The minimum age for employment is fourteen, but the Ministry of Labor, which has the responsibility of enforcing labor laws, rarely prosecutes violations of the minimum-age regulation; young street vendors or windshield cleaners are a common sight in Managua, and children frequently work on family farms at a young age.

A National Minimum Wage Commission establishes minimum wages for different sectors of the economy. Enforcement of the minimum wage is lax, however many workers are paid less than the law allows. But, in reality the minimum wage is so low that many workers need to make well above the set amount to survive. Labor groups have argued that the minimum wage is inadequate to feed a family of four, and in 1992 the country's largest umbrella group of unions issued a statement demanding that the government tie the minumum wage to the cost of living

A new labor code was ceated in 1996 which seems to foreshadow an inprovement in labor conditions and the rights of workers. The main problem is that most of Nicaraguan laborers are unskilled and a dime a dozen. Lack of adequate training is a major problem. This does create an abundance of low-cost labor.

Under the most recent legislation Nicaraguan workers are required to make up at least 90% of any labor force. The workweek is 48 hours over six days with anything over that being considered overtime. There are about 10 unpaid holidays yearly and an employee is entitled to 30 days vacation for each 12 months that they spend working. They can chose to trade in 15 of those days for cash payment. Employers are also required to pay benefits which total almost half of their actual salaries. Severance pay must be provided with the worker entitled to a certain portion of his salary for each year that he has worked as wel as his bonuses, provided he was not fired for misconduct.

Employees are given a maxium of 30 days leave for illness and the period may be renewed and can stretch up to a year for serious disabilities. Women are given 84 days paid maternity leave. if an employee works overtime, he is entitled to twice the regular pay, and if the employer is late in payment, an extra 10% of the amount owed must be added to the total salary each week. The Ministry of Labor arbitrates when there are disputes between employees and the employer.

Below we have listed the detailed version of the labor code. However, we suggest you consult your attorney if you questions about it or when there is a problem with an employee to avoid misunderstandings.

It important to know that many jobs are done on a contract basis. This way the employer isn't responsible for many benefits. We know an expat who is remodeling a beautiful colonial home in Granada. He has a crew of five or six laborers and a foreman. All of his workers are under contract. However, don't assume that all employees can be hired on a contract basis. Again, it it best to check with a lawyer to find out about your reponsibilities as an employer.

Nicaragua's Labor Law

Nicaragua''s labor laws for domestic workers are strict and difficult to interpret.

Investors should consider the following :

* abundant low-cost labor
* labor is primarily unskilled
* nine to ten paid holidays per year
* required severance pay
* weakening power of unions
* minimum wage raised November 1, 1997

In December of 1996, a new Labor Code took effect, replacing the outdated 1944 version. The changes represent a significant compromise between the business community and unions, foreshadowing an improvement in labor relations.

AVAILABILITY OF LABOR

Nicaragua's labor force is estimated to be at 1.7 million. Of the economically active population, 40 percent are employed in the agricultural sector, 15 percent in the manufacturing sector, and 45 percent in the service sector. Considering that

SAVING MONEY IN NICARAGUA

the unemployment rate stood at 16 percent in 1996 and the underemployment rate at 36 percent according to government estimates, the availability of unskilled labor is significant. One drawback is the shortage of skilled technicians and managerial personnel. However, the numbers are improving with the return of exiled members of the business and professional classes.

WORK SHIFTS AND REST PERIODS

Shifts

There is a maximum 48hr work week consisting of six 8-hour days. However, on mutual agreement of employee and employer, alternate schedules may be worked (for example five 9.6 hour days) within the 48hr weekly limit. For areas considered unhealthy, there is a maximum 6 hour shift per day, for night shifts, 7 hours, and swing shifts, 7 1/2 hours. Overtime refers to any time that exceeds these limits. In addition, for every regular shift there is to be a 1/2 hour paid break for employees.

Vacation Leave

All employees are entitled to 30 calendar days vacation for every 12 months worked for the same employer. While employees may forego 15 of those days in return for a cash payment, 15 days must be taken as actual vacation.

Rest Days

For every six consecutive days worked there is to be a seventh day of rest.

Holidays

Official holidays include:
* New Year's Day: January 1
* Holy Thursday
* Good Friday
* Labor Day: May 1
* Battle of San Jacinto: September 14

* Independence Day: September 15
* Immaculate Conception Day: December 8
* Christmas Day: December 25
In Managua, official holidays also include:
* Festival of Santo Domingo: August 1 and 10

The government or municipality holds the right to announce any other official holidays where employers are required to pay salaries.

SALARIES AND OTHER PAYROLL CONSIDERATIONS

Minimum Wage

Minimum wages were raised on November 1, 1997. However, the following minimum wages are lower than what most employees earn.

Sector	Monthly Minimum Wage*
Manufacturing	51.02
Transportation	45.91
Construction	48.97
Mines	61.22
Utilities Financial Institutions	71.42
Agriculture	30.61
Services	47.95

*In US$ based on an exchange rate of 12.8 córdobas/1.00

Average Wages The following table represents the average wage for the various sectors as calculated by INSS, the social security system.

SAVING MONEY IN NICARAGUA

Sector	Monthly Wage*
Manufacturing	183.95
Transportation	292.14
Construction	166.81
Mines	229.43
Utility	242.01
Financial Institutions	298.51
Agriculture	119.23
Services	133.53

*In US$ based on an exchange rate of 12.8 cordobas/1.00

Payroll Burden

In addition to base salaries, the labor law requires employers to pay other benefits which total approximately 46.86 percent of the wage as shown below. In addition to this amount the employer must take into consideration the costs of severance pay.

Payroll Burden (annualized)

Concept	Description	Percent
Annual Vacations	30 paid days	8.33%
Christmas bonus	1 month's salary	8.33%

Seventh Day	1 for every 6 days	12.05%
Paid Holidays	10 days (appx.)	3.65%
Social Security (urban)	employer's contribution	12.50%
INATEC	training	2.00%
Total		**46.86%**

Annual Vacation

Employers have to pay their employees the equivalent of 30 days paid vacation for a full year's work regardless of whether the employee takes the full 30 days or substitutes 15 days for a cash payment.

Christmas Bonus

The Labor Code requires all employees be paid a salary for the "13th month," the equivalence of a Christmas bonus. The amount is based upon the salary paid for the month of November.

Seventh Day

Salaries are to be given for the seventh day or day of rest according to the Labor Code. This is true only after having worked for 6 days. The salary is based upon the wages set in the contract. If, for example, wages are paid on an hourly basis, the seventh day counts as an 8 hour work day. If salaries are given upon a task or production, then the pay rate is equal to the average task or production rate for that week.

Paid Holidays

Depending on the municipality, there are approximately 10 days considered holidays where employees are to be given a paid day of rest.

SAVING MONEY IN NICARAGUA

Social Security: (3 types)

In Nicaragua, employers are required to contribute to the social security system. There are three types of social security:

INTEGRAL-This is the type of social security provided to urban laborers. In this case, the employer contributes the equivalent of 12.5 percent of the employees salary to cover social security costs while the employee pays the social security system 4 percent.

IVM- This IVM is required typically for laborers in rural areas. In this case, the employer is responsible for 5 percent to cover social security costs while the employee is responsible for 2 percent.

SELF-EMPLOYED- In this case the individual contributes 13.5 percent of his or her salary.

INATEC

Employers are required to pay 2% to the National Institute for Technology (INATEC) per employee for training purposes.

Other Considerations

Severance Pay

At the termination of a labor contract, the employer is required to pay 1 month's salary for each of the first three years worked and 20 day's salary for each year up to a maximum of five months. The employee is also entitled to his or her salary for vacation time and the 13th month in proportion to the amount of time worked at the time of dismissal. This holds true even if the reason for termination is based on mutual consensus or if the employee quits. If fired for an unjust cause, then the employee is also entitled to a month's salary for white collar workers and 15 days salary for blue collar workers. In the event of an extraordinary cause for the termination of a labor contract, such as destruction of property or theft on part of the employee, the employer is only required to pay for the relevant vacation time and 13th month.

Sickness Benefits and Accident Compensation

Employees are to be given a maximum of 30 days leave in case of illness. In the case of partial disability, the employee is entitled to leave of up to six months, or a year if he/she is permanently disabled. For maternity, women are given 84 days of maternity leave. INSS will cover 60% of the salary in case of illness, varying rates for disability, and will also pay for the maternity leave. The employer has no obligation except forthe rate (i.e. 12.5%) it already pays to the social security system for each employee.

Over-time

Over-time is to be paid at twice the regular rate set in the labor contract.

Payment Delays

If payment to the employee is delayed, the employer is required to pay an extra 10 percent of what is owed for every late week.

LABOR ENVIRONMENT

Addressing Grievances

Grievances can be made by a single employee, a group of employees, or through a union. Grievances are to be first directed to the employer and then to the Ministry of Labor.

MINISTRY OF LABOR

The Ministry of Labor has the right to suspend the activities of a firm if it is infringing upon the rights of its employees as defined in the Labor Code.

STRIKES

Under the new Labor Code, strikes may not take place until all other possible measures have been taken to resolve the dispute. That includes exhausting all conciliatory measures provided bythe Ministry of Labor. If these requirements are not fulfilled, the strike is considered illegal, inwhich the employer has the right to dismiss any employee who does not return to work. If a strike is considered legal, then the employer may not hire new workers throughout the durationof the strike, nor terminate any labor contracts.

Collective Bargaining

Collective bargaining, a written agreement between employers and employees, can only take place between an employer and a union.

Unions

* Labor unions must have at least 20 members and they must register with the Ministry of Labor.

* Membership in both Sandinista and non-Sandinista unions has declined in recent years and continues to fall. Today, less than half (and perhaps as few as 1/3) of workers in the formal sector are unionized. The political power of both Sandinista and non-Sandinista unions has diminished accordingly. Additionally, Sandinista unions have been without the benefit of direct government support since the Sandinistas lost power in 1990, and have been wracked by charges of corruption. Just over half of unionized workers are members of Sandinista unions. Many employers find non-Sandinista unions easier to work with than Sandinista unions.

Hiring and Firing Requirements

* Employers are required to have a labor force comprised of at least 90% Nicaraguans.

* Employers must obtain permission from the Labor Ministry to dismiss a group of employees(i.e. when closing down a plant). Permission is not necessary when firing 1 or 2 employees as long as they are given their due compensation and 30 day notice prior to dismissal.

It is best to consult with your lawyer so he can explain the nuances of the country's labor law.

Courtesy of the American Embassy in Managua

Health Care

Staying Healthy

Unlike some countries in Latin America, especially Mexico, Nicaragu's tap water supply is good and perfectly safe to drink. In most towns and cities you can drink without the fear of Montezuma's Revenge (diarrhea) or other intestinal problems. However, be careful when you drink water in the countryside. But if you prefer, bottled water is available. And you're probably better off drinking it. Becareful of ice cubes since they are sometimes made of contaminated water. You should be careful about eating unpeeled raw foods, and meats. Wash and peel all fresh fruits and vegetables. Avoid drinking fruit drinks made with water that are sold in stands on the street. You should also watch out for raw seafood dishes, like ceviche , served in some bars and restaurants.You should make sure to cook all raw foods.

Hospital Bautista is a full-service institution.

SAVING MONEY IN NICARAGUA

Nicaragua's health care system is ranked 70th in the world by by the World Health Organization and ahead of many of the other countries in Latin America. It its ranked ahead of Argentina, Guatemala, Panamá, Brazil, Boliva, and Peru.

The country's health conditions are improving, although it remains a tropical country with the presence of malaria, dengue fever and a variety of gastro-intestinal disorders. Typhoid and gamma globulina (or Hepatitis A) are recommended vaccinations prior to spending an extended stay in Nicaragua.

Local hospitals are adequate for basic care. However, they fall short of U.S. standards and are not recommended for serious conditions. Public hospitals can be crowded at times with long waits to get medical attention. Private clinics are a better bet but more expensive than public facilities. There are a number of U.S. - trained physicains in the country.

The **Hospital Bautista** is affliiated with Baptist Health Systems of South Florida, P.O. Box 709, Managua Nicaragua, Tel: (505) 249-7070 or 249-7277 Fax: (505) 249-7327, E-mail: info@bhospital.org.ni or direchb@ibw.com.ni. This hospital is a non-profit institution which was founded in 1930.

The outpatient and inpatient center include care in all medical and surgical specialities: arthroscopy, Bronchoscopy, cardiology, Cat scan, Dentistry, Dermatology, ears nose and throat treatment, emergency medical care,general surgery, endoscopy, gynecology, obstetrics, hemotology, oncology, internal medicine, pediatric care, plastic and reconstructive surgery, psychiatry, ultrasound, urology and more.

The hospital has an experienced medical and backup staff available 24 hours a day. The hospital operates its own ambulance service. High quality patient care is guaranteed by qualified professional nurses. Several medical plans are offered by Baptist Hospital with coverage at different levels (private and national Social Security Institute INSS).

Hospital Alejandro Dávila Bolaños (222-2764) is another good private hospital. Other hospitals in Managua are as follows: **Hospital Monte España** (278-3920 or 278-3921), **Hospital Salud Integral** (266-1707 or 266-0172), **Carlos Marx Hospital** (248-2260) **Berta Calderon Hospital** (260-1303), **Manolo Morales Hospital** (277-0990) and **Psychiatria Hospital** (266-7877).

Please see the Nicaraguan telephone book for more listings.

Some well-to-do Nicaraguans and many Americans go to Costa Rica for specialized medical care. Recently the ex-head of Nicaragua's army, Humberto Ortega, chose to have heart surgery at the Clínica Bíbilica in Costa Rica.

In Costa Rica the **Clinica Bíblica** (Tel:257-5252, Fax:255-4947, E-mail:asoserme@racsa.co.cr,

The new Japanese hospital on the outskirts of Granada.

SAVING MONEY IN NICARAGUA

www.edenia.com/medical/biblica), in downtown San José, is now affiliated with the Blue Cross Blue Shield network. It is a first-class private hospital with an excellent coronary unit. This fine hospital is staffed with doctors who are highly trained. Complete hospital services as well as lab work are available.

Dental Care

You will find the cost of dental work affordable in Nicaragua.

In Managua try **Policlinica Odontológico Mauricio Abdalah R.** (265-1648, 265-2144 or 265-0512). They offer a full range of dental services and are open 24-hours. If you are looking for a dentist contact : **Dr. Carlos A. Bustos** at Tel: (505) 552-2781, E-mail: betocab@hotmail.com. His practice is located in Granada and he specializes in general odontology services. Some wealthier Nicaraguans and foreigners travel to Costa Rica for special dental services.

If you decide to travel to neighboring Costa Rica for your dental work, contact Doctors **Themla Rubinstein** and **Josef Cordero Pinchanski**. They are an experienced dental team who have traditionally offered quality dental care. They both graduated from the University of Costa Rica in General Dentistry and have studied in Switzerland, Canada and Germany.Together they have provided 18 years of dental care and services to local and foreign patients, including adults, teenagers and children.

Their services include implants, gum treatment, root canals, bleaching, oral surgery, crowns, bridges and nitrous oxide sedation. They specialize in working with Swiss porcelain and create porcelain veneers, crown , inlays, onlays, pure porcelain bridges and braces. This goes hand-in-hand with their mercury-free dentistry and outstanding customer service.

Doctors Cordero and Rubinstein provide fast service with quality workmanship and have their own on-site laboratory you can be sure to get the best job without having to leave the premises.

For more information, their state-of-the-art facility is located on Paseo Colón across from the Cine Universal on the second floor. You can also reach them at (506) 257-8856, Fax (506) 255-2004 or their e-mail at: dental@racsa.co.cr. Please visit their web site at: www.cosmetic-dentistry.com.

Pharmacies

Most pharmacies (*farmacias*) in Nicaragua carry adequate supplies of most commonly use medicines , but some kinds of prescription medications may not be available or be very expensive. We suggest you bring any special medicines from the States or Canada. We know of a couple of Americans who go to neighboring Costa Rica to get certain medicines which are not available in Nicaragua.

A full-service Nicaraguan Pharmacy

The **Hospital Bautista** (249-7277 ext. 4605) in Managua, offers a complete stock of medicine and will fill prescriptions 24 hours a day. Other pharmacies in Managua are **Centro Eckerd** (278-0367), **Farmacia Medco** (266-8018) and **Farmacia Sama** (265-1796). **Super Farmacia Alemana** (249-7659, 249-5292) is open 24-hours daliy.

Farmacia Xolotlan (266-5555 or 266-5088) has free delivery as does **Farmacia Xoraimita** (522-5915).

Two excellent laboratories are **Hospital Bautista** (249-7070) and **Bioanálisis** (278-6350).

Cosmetic Surgery

While living in Nicaragua you can find the "Fountain of Youth" having cosmetic surgery. Please contact **Dr. Rommel Mendieta** at Centro de Cirugía Plástica, Tel: (505) 270- 4464 or (505) 270-5598, E-mail: remdiet@ibw.ni or see www.demendieta.com.

One quick word about cosmetic surgery in Nicaragua or anywhere in Latin America. To get the best results from your surgery we suggest you do the following: (1) Ask the U.S. Embassy for a list a certified plastic surgeons. (2) Also check with the Colegio de Médicos (the local equivalent of the A.M.A.) to see if a particular doctor is a real plastic surgeon. (3) Ask a local family doctor for a recommendation of a good plastic surgeon. (4) Talk with former patients of the doctor of your choice before you make a decision. Find out if they are pleased with the results of their surgery.

Doctor's List

Here is a partial list of doctors. For additional names please see the phone book or talk to other expats.

In Managua:
Dra. Luz Cantillo Olivares (Dermatology) 249-0608
Dr. Enrique Medina Sandino (Endocrinology) 268-0031
Dr. Fletcher Gurdian (Gastroenterology) 278-1310
Dra Doris Aguilar (Gynecology) 266-0818
Dr. Noe Larios Delgadillo (General Medicine) 249-7070 Ext.178
Dr César A. Vargas (Orthopedic) 266-9557
Dr. Roberto López (Nose, Ear and Throat) 222-3745
Dr. Luis Fonseca Espinoza (Pediatics) 266-2192
Dr. Allan Lacayo (Uroology) 266-0810

In Granada:
Dr. Eddy Rose B 552-4867
Dr. Eli R. Soza 552-3276
Dr. Edgard Vallejos 552-2245
Dr. Mario Hernández 552-6354
Dra. Giselda Espinoza 552-2363
Dra. Martha Dolla Abarca 552-3276

Care for the Eldery

Since hired help is so inexpensive you can hire a full-time domestic to take care of an infirm person. A full-time maid to take care of a sick or elerly person shouldn't cost more than $75.00 monthly.

Money

Nicaragua's currency is the *córdoba*, named for one of the Spanish conquerors and the city of Cordova from where he came. The *córdoba* is divided into 100 centavos. Bills come in denominations of 1/2 (50 *centavos*), 1, 5, 10, 50, and 100 córdobas. Colloquially you may hear prices given in *pesos*, which is another word for *córdobas*. Don't let it confuse you. The *córdoba* is undergoing a fixed devaluatuion. You may find exchange rates published in most local Central American newspapers.

The rate of exchange as of September 2000 was 12.80 *córdobas* for one U.S. dollar.

SAVING MONEY IN NICARAGUA

Banking

Nicaragua has both state owned and private banks. The private banking sector was re-established in 1991, twelve years after being nationalized by the Sandinista Regime. The Private Bank law of 1991 created the **Superintendencia de Bancos** to oversee the operations of the private and state-owned banks. The Superintendency conducts on-site inspections of each bank twice monthly.

The **Banco Central de Nicaragua** (Central Bank) Tel; (505) 265-2051, Fax: (505) 265-2272, www.bcn.gob.ni handles foreign enchange and investor incentives.

Banco Nacional de Desarollo Tel: (505) 227-5310 and **Banco de Industria y Comercio** Tel: (505) 276-2730 are two state-owned banks.

Banco Mercantil Tel: (505) 266-8226 , **Banco de la Producción** Tel: (505) 278-2508, **Banco de Expotación** (BANEXPO) Tel: (505) 278-7171 and **BanCentro** Tel: (505) 278-2777 are the country's most important private banks. Bancentro has correspondent banks in the United States including CitiBank of New York.

Bancentro offers a full-service bank in Granada

They also offer debit cards which can be used at ATMs around the country. To find out more about this excellent bank access www.bancentro.com.ni.

If you plan to reside in Granada we suggest you contact Leonel Poveda Sediles at **Bancentro**. He speaks fluent English and will help you set up an account. However, to open almost any type of a bank account you have to be a resident, own property or prove you permanently rent a house in the city.

One bit of good news for seniors. If you are over 60 years old you don't have to wait in a bank line. You have the right to go right to the front of the line.

Banks are usually open weekdays from 8am to noon and from 1pm to 4:30pm. Some are open on Saturdays to noon. Traveler's checks may be cashed at any bank as well as Casa de Cambios. You may also change money with cambistas or money changers who hang out in the central area of most towns.

Taxes

A new tax law went into effect in May, 1997. The law was designed to reduce tax evasion by specifying those items that are exempt from tax payments and abolishing the government officials' discretion to make exceptions to the law or exonerate tariffs. It also aims at promoting investment and overall economic growth through a series of changes favorable to businesses.

PRINCIPAL TAXES
National
1. Income Taxes
2. Consumption Tax (Luxury Tax)
3. General Sales Tax

SAVING MONEY IN NICARAGUA

4. Social Security Taxes
5. Import Tariff
6. Temporary Protection Tax
Municipal
1. Sales Tax
2. Territorial and Residence Tax

CLASSES OF TAX PAYERS

1. Persons or associations of persons
2. Incorporated associations of persons
   a. Corporations (sociedades anonimas (S.A.), societies, associations and foundations
   b. Mixed corporations (i.e. government with private capital)
   c. State entities and state-owned enterprises

Each of these is subject to income taxes and the sales tax regardless of nationality as long as the source of that income is based in Nicaragua.

TAX YEAR

July 1 - June 30 and special periods for seasonal activities.

FREE TRADE ZONE

The free trade zones were authorized to encourage job creation. Under the Free-trade Zones Law, companies are granted full exemption from income taxes for the first 10 years and 60 percent exemption thereafter. The free trade zones are also exempt from import duties, levies, and sales taxes on imports. Currently, the large, state owned "Las Mercedes" free trade zone is located near Managua's international airport and a smaller "Index" free trade zone is located off of Managua's north highway. Four other private free trade zones have been authorized, but havenot yet been opened.

INCOME TAXES

For individuals, income taxes are calculated through a progressive tax rate as income increases. Taxable income is based on Nicaraguan-source income. The maximum rate applicable is 30%. This tax rate will fall to 25% in July, 1999.

For a corporation and other associations, there is a flat rate of 30% on Nicaraguan-source income. Beginning July 1999, this flat rate will be reduced to 25%.

Land or assets may can also be taxed as income. For the agricultural sector, there is a tax per lot of land in excess of some specified amount. This amount depends on the region. For all other sectors, individuals who do not receive a salary but are engaged in a professional activity will betaxed 1.5 percent on the value of their tangible assets or inventories in excess of 500,000 *córdobas* obtained that year.

Key Deductions Include:

* costs associated with the production process such as rent, insurance, advertising, etc.

* losses due to bad debts

* interest paid on a debt as long as it was used for investment or production.

* losses due to destruction or loss of assets used in the production process if they are not insured

* the amount needed to replace depreciating capital

* donations to certain specified groups

* benefits for employees directed towards their well-being such as medical services

* insurance for employees up to 10% of their salaries

SAVING MONEY IN NICARAGUA

For deductions, the income tax payer must document and register with Ministry of Finance all costs being claimed. Income tax is not to be paid on capital gains or interest earned from the local stock exchange or from dividends.

CONSUMPTION TAX (Impuesto Especifico del Consumo-IEC)

The consumption tax is applicable to non-essential items. The IEC will be based on the sale price of the producer.

Exempt from the IEC are raw materials, intermediate goods, and capital goods necessary for theproduction process. Petroleum has its own consumption tax.

Credit for the IEC paid is possible:

* when the goods acquired or services performed are necessary for the production process

* for deductible goods and services under income taxes

GENERAL SALES TAX (Impuesto General al Valor-IGV)

The IGV, a 15% tax, is applicable to most transfers of goods and services. However, it is important to note that the new law has eliminated the IGV for several activities. Article 1, 13, 14, and 17 of the new tax law for a list of these activities.

Also, retainers of the IGV must withhold 5% when paying for professional activities.

Credit for the IGV paid is possible:

* when the goods acquired or services performed are necessary for the production process

* for deductible goods and services under income taxes

SOCIAL SECURITY: (3 types)

INTEGRAL-This is the type of social security provided to urban employees. In this case, the employer contributes the equivalent of 12.5 percent of the employees salary to cover social security costs while the employee pays the social security system 4 percent.

The IVM is required typically for laborers in rural areas. In this case, the employer is responsiblefor 5 percent to cover social security costs while the employee is responsible for 2 percent.

SELF-EMPLOYED- In this case the individual contributes 13.5 percent of his or her salary.

IMPORT TARIFF (Derechos Arancelarios a la Importacion or DAI) This is the principal form of taxation for imports under the Tariff System of Central America.

(DAI). The DAI varies depending on the item. There have been some modifications to DAI as found in Annex B of the new tax law of May 1997.

TEMPORARY PROTECTIVE TARRIFF (Arancel Temporal de Proteccion or ATP)

The ATP is a replacement for the previous Stamp Tax (ITF). It is applicable to the CIF value of all imported items. The tariff will equal 5% except for those items found in Annex 1 and 2 of the new law. The ATP will be phased out by January 1, 1999. All other items in the annexes that will still have a tariff above 0% by January 1, 2000 will be reduced 5% every 6 months until it reaches 0%.

MODIFICATION OF MUNICIPIAL INCOME TAX

In January of 1998, the municipal income tax will be reduced from 2% to 1.5%. In January 2000 it will be reduced to 1.0%.

OTHER REGULATIONS ON EXPORTS AND IMPORTS

Non-tariff barriers are not allowed under the new law for exports and imports unless these barriers are in place for the protection of public health, sanitation, the environment, security or for a national emergency. Exporters will be given compensation for taxes paid on imports beginning January 1,

1998. The compensation is 1.5% on the FOB value of all exports. For those benefiting from the Free Trade Zone, the compensation will only be applicable to raw materials, intermediate goods, and capital goods.

All payment of taxes, permits and licenses for exports will be eliminated.

TAX ADMINISTRATION and PROCEDURES
MINISTRY OF FINANCE

The Ministry of Finance has the right to establish procedures for customs and fiscal control.

DIRECCION GENERAL DE INGRESOS (DGI)

The DGI is a branch of the Ministry of Finance. IT is responsible for the administration and collection of taxes.

WHEN ARE TAX RETURNS DUE?

Tax returns are due within the first three months of the next fiscal year for personal activities and various sectors. However, for the industrial, commercial, agricultural sectors and others, tax returns may be due when the companies accounting period is over, as long as it is previously arranged with the Direccion General de Ingresos. For those that are planning to leave the country, tax returns are due prior to departure.

All corporations or individuals earning an excess of 50,000 *córdobas*, even if they are exempt from taxes, must file a tax return with the Direccion General de Ingresos.

For deductions it is necessary that the income tax payer document and register all costs being claimed. For credit for IGV or IEC paid, it is necessary that the tax payer present written proof (i.e.receipts).

PAYMENT AND COLLECTION FOR CORPORATIONS

Corporations are required to declare and pay the appropriate IGV and a 1% tax on sales each month. The 1%

tax is credited to the total income tax owed at the end of the fiscal year.

WITHHOLDING TAXES FROM EMPLOYEES

It is the obligation of the firm to withhold monthly the relevant amount of taxes from the employees paycheck who earn an excess of 50,000 cordobas annually. The amount to be withheld should be determined according to the following chart.

Taxable Income From C$	To C$:*	Tax Base	Applicable Percentage	On an excess of:
1	50,000	-	0%	0
50,001	100,000	-	10%	50,000
100,001	200,000	5,000	15%	100,000
200,001	300,000	20,000	20%	200,000
300,001	400,000	40,000	25%	300,000
400,001	and up..	65,000	30%	400,000
*Córdobas				

The employer must notify the Direccion General de Ingresos during the first 15 days of the fiscal year of all employees who fit the previous description. The firm is then to proceed by presenting the income earned of all of these employees.

The firm is also under the obligation to refund any excess amount withheld.

CALCULATIONS

Depreciation

* Depreciation must be calculated by the straight line method.

* It is permitted for tax payers to choose to shorten the lifetime of assets and rate of depreciation as long as the amount does not exceed the original value of the piece of equipment.

1.5% tax on assets exceeding 500,000 cordobas

* Do not include the value of the home, the vehicle for personal use, or items used in the home.

* The value of assets will be based on the cost of acquisition or construction, minus depreciation

and/or the cost of production or acquisition of inventories.

TAX AUDITS

The DGI has the right to conduct tax audits whenever it deems it necessary. If there is suspicion of tax evasion, it has the right to temporarily or permanently close the plant, business, etc.

APPEALS

Appeals can be directed to the DGI or a commission created by the Ministry of Finance.

STATUTE OF LIMITATIONS

When an individual or company fails to pay taxes that were withheld (i.e. 15% IGV on sales), then there is no statute of limitations. If however, an individual or company fails topay their income tax, then the limit is 7 years.

As proof of that commitment, in 1999 the National Assembly passed an amendment to the "Ley de Justicia Tributaria" (Tax Justice Law), which will provide additional tax reductions.

Courtesy of the U.S.Embassy in Managua

Tax Protection

In general taxes are relatively low in Nicaragua. The Administración de Rentas (In Granada call 552-2946) is Nicaragua's version of the I.R.S. However, they are far less efficient. As previously mentioned if you go into tourism there are many incentive which may reduce your tax obligations.

Foreign income is exempt from taxation in Nicaragua. You will have to pay taxes on income earned in Nicargua. However, if you go into business in Nicaragua and form a tax sheltered corporation, many of your expenses can be written off.

Don't panic! A good accountant or one of the lawyers we list in the guide can help you minimize your taxes and avoid problems later on.

You form *Sociedad Anónima*, to shelter your earnings. Some foreigners choose to set up these types of corporations while many don't. Briefly, a *Sociedad Anónima* is an anonymous corporation you can set up without their names appearing on any records. The initials S.A. will appear after a corporation's name instead of Inc. A Nicaraguan corporation is similar to its U.S. counterpart in having a board of directors, shareholders and shares which can be bought and sold freely. You control all the stock in the corporation but your identity remains unknown. This way you're able to maintain some degree of secrecy in financial matters and protect yourself from some tax problems.

These offshore corporations are used in most business transactions within Nicaragua and abroad. Because they are foreign corporations they are not subject to U.S. taxes.

There are additional benefits to establishing an "offshore" corporation in any Latin American country. If you put your property in your corporation's name, it is easier to transfer title. All that is involved is the exchange of the company's stocks. This way your assets can be transferred or sold by simply giving your shares to the new owner or visa versa. Owning one of these corporations entitles you to start a business and open a checking account in the company's name even though you are not a legal resident or citizen.

If you have relatives on the the board of directors of your company, there will be no probate taxes in case of your demise.

SAVING MONEY IN NICARAGUA

It is well-nigh impossible to find out whose name appears in the public records since ownership is confidential. Furthermore, if you get involved in any serious litigation it will be difficult to sue you directly. You will be protected against most judgements and liens. This affords your assets greater protection. If you are a non-resident foreigner you must have one of these corporations to own a business.

Contact your attorney if you are seriously thinking about forming one of these anonymous corporations. Your lawyer can explain how these corporations work and why they have advantages and disadvantages. The fee for starting one of these corporations is usually between $500 and $1000. It will usually take a few months to finish all of the paperwork depending on how fast your lawyer works.

Be forewarned: A corporation's secrecy is not "foolproof." If you attempt to use your corporation for fraudulent purposes, you are asking for big trouble. Fortunately the IRS usually won't go after you unless you are a "big fish" who has done something obvious to attract their attention.

If you desire better protection for your assets or business we suggest you form a Panamanian corporation. We don't know all of the nuances of setting up one of these corporations, we suggest you contact one of the companies listed at the end of the next section.

You must file your U.S. income tax returns yearly through the American Embassy. You have to declare all income earned abroad but you may claim a tax exemption up to $74,000 on overseas-earned income. The $74,000 applies to individual, unmarried taxpayers. If you are married, you and your spouse may exclude up to $144,000 of foreign income, but you cannot combine the two exemptions. You must reside outside of the U.S. for at least 330 days a year or be a legal resident of a foreign country to qualify for this exemption. Your primary business must also be located abroad to qualify for the foreign-earned imcome exemption. Fortunately, if you live outside the U.S. you may wait to file your taxes until June 15th. You need to use a U.S. tax form 2555 to apply for this exemption.

Even if you earn no income in Nicaragua, it is imperative to file a standard 1040 tax form to avoid problems. Payment of taxes, interest and penalties can now be done by credit card by dialing **1-888-2PAY-TAX.**

If you have any tax questions, contact the U.S. Embassy or IRS. Call either the Consular Section of the U.S. Embassy, 266-6010 / 266-6018 or the nearest IRS office in Mexico City at 525 211-0042, ext. 3557. You may consult the IRS Web site at: www.irs.gov. There is also book titled *The Expats Guide to U.S. Taxes*. It may be purchased through www.amazon.com.

Canadians will have to contact the local Canadian Consulate at 268-1983 concerning their tax obligations while living abroad.

Forming A Panamanian (Offshore) Corporation

Offshore corporations enable you to act as an international citizen with complete confidentiality, privacy and safety. Offshore corporations can legally open Offshore bank accounts, brokerage accounts, hold credit cards, own property, stocks etc. and in many cases completely exempt you from any tax reporting requirements and with complete confidentiality.

WHY PANAMA?

For many years Pamana has been recognized worldwide as a major international offshore banking center offering very attractive legal and tax incentives to Panamanian corporations. For example, Panamaian law allows Panamanian corporations to issue "bearer" stock certificates. This means the owners who control the corporation do not have to be named in any public record, since ownership is through physical possession of the "bearer" shares. Panamanian Corporations are not subject to Panamanian tax on income earned outside of Panama. Also, unlike Nicaragua and Costa Rica, Panama allows you to name your corporationn with an English name, which has many advanyages when using your Panamanian Corporation in English speaking countries. These are just a few of the more important reasons why Panamanian corproations are so popular.

FORMING A PANAMANIAN CORPORATION:

First we recommend you select a name in English followed by: Corp., Corporation Inc. or Incorporated. You cannot use the words Bank, Trust, Foundation or Insurance in the name of your corporation. You may use any name as long as it is not being currently used in Panama. If you own a U.S. Corporation, you may find some advantages in using the same name for your Panamanian corporation, if available in Panama. This would allow you to have identically named offshore and onshore bank accounts as well as other similar advantages.

Panamanian corporations are typically formed with nominee directors, president, secretary and treasure. These are Panamanian citizens who are modestly paid officer workers. If you wish, you may select your own directors and officers. However, the original directors and officers selected are registered with the Panamanian public registry which becomes public information available to anyone who inquires. Thereofore, if you wish confidentiality, we recommend you select the nominee director option. Officers and directors can always be changed later.

Panamanian law allows corporate shares to be issued in "bearer" form. This means that whoever physically possesses the shares, owns the company. This allows for total confidentiality of ownership, since the person who physically possesses the shares is not identified in any public or even private record. Having a Panamanian corporation with "bearer" shares also makes transfer of ownership completely private and not a matter of public record, since transfer of ownership is a simple process of physically transferring the "bearer" shares to a new owner. It is very similar to passing a $20 bill to someone else versus writing them a check. This feature makes it very easy to sell or transfer properties confidentially by simply transferring the "bearer" shares and ownership of the Panamanian corporation and thus avoiding many forms of taxes and closing costs because title to the property remains in the name of the Panamanian corporation. Essentially you are simply selling the corporation which owns the property.

Your Panamanian Corporation comes with a notarized General Power of Attorney (in English) signed by two officers named in the articles of incorporation. This power of attorney provides a blank space for you to fill in the name of any person you want to act as the legal agent for the corporation with the authority to open and sign on corporate bank accounts, enter into contracts for the corporation, sign and transfer assets for the corporation, etc. Although you fill in your name or another person name as having Power of Attorney, this is not evidence of ownership. The person named is simply an agent, similar to an employee empowered to act for the corporation. You may order as many additonal Power of Attorney forms as you wish.

As you can see there is a world market for Panamanian corporations because they are extremely popular. Older Panamanian corporations with established bank accounts sell for thousands of dollars or more. Selling your Panamanian corporation is a matter of physically transferring the "bearer" stock certificate together with the other corporate records to

Protect Your Assets by Forming a Panamanian Corporation as mentioned in this book

- Reduce your tax liability.
- Your corporation can operate in Panama and Worldwide.
- Ownership remains anonymous.
- Corporations offer freedom, flexibility and are easy to operate.
- Transfer assets to heirs.
- Bank account for inmediate use with ATM Card and International Master Card linked to the account.
- And many more advantages.

For additional information contact us at:
Relocation, Investment and Retirement Consultants
E-mail: panamaniancorps@hotmail.com
Fax: 011-506-261-8968
www.liveincostarica.com
(click on consulting services and then Panamanian Corporations)

Relocation, Retirement and Investment Consultants

Helping newcomers find SUCCESS and HAPPINESS in Costa Rica for over 15 years. We offer absolutely the BEST network of contacts and INSIDER information available in Costa Rica.

- Panamanian and Costa Rican confidential corporations to protect your assets.
- Affordable Cosmetic Surgery.
- Expert legal advice (The best legal minds in Costa Rica).
- How to really make money in Costa Rica and high-yielding tax-free investments up to 25% annually (2% or more monthly in dollars).
- Find-a-rental (assistance locating affordable rentals in prime locations)
- Immigration matters and residency.
- TAILOR-MADE BILINGUAL TOURS FOR INDIVIDUALS AND COUPLES.
- Moving household goods.
- Sure-fire safe business ideas, advice and contacts.
- Real estate (The best brokers in Costa Rica).
- How to form fool-proof offshore corporations to protect your assents
- Where to make friends and how to keep busy and happy.
- How and where to find love and romance.
- Opening and bank account and safety deposit box.
- Internet hook-up.
- The quickest and best ways to learn Spanish (secrets time-tested methods).
- Private mail service to the U.S.
- Buying and insuring a car.
- Plus all of the ins and outs and dos and don'ts of living in Costa Rica and so much more.

Satisfaction Guaranteed!

Let the experts save you a lot of HEADACHES and MONEY by contacting us today at: E-mail: crbooks@racsa.co.cr
PLEASE SEE: www.liveincostarica.com / www.costaricabooks.com
Suite 1 SJO 981 P.O. Box: 025216. Miami, FL 33102-5216
Be sure to ask about our daily rates, one day free weekly packages, group discounts, informative seminars and special retainers.

the new owner.

The one-time cost for setting up a simple Panamanian Corporstion is around $1300. You will have to pay an annual Registered Agent and Director's fee of $295 yearly, due one month before the anniversary date of the corporation.

For additonal information about starting a Panamanian corporation contact: **Relocation and Retirement Consultants**, Suite 1 SJO 981, P.O. Box 025216 (SJO-316), Miami, FL 33102 Fax: 011-(506) 261-8968, E-mail: crbooks@racsa.co.cr 24 hrs. www.liveincostarica.com or www.liveinnicaragua.com.

Insurance

The size of the insurance market in Nicaragua is small according to the latest report of **Nicaraguan Bank Superintendency** (the regulatory body for banks, insurance companies and bonded warehouses).

There is a total of five insurance companies. **INISER**, Apartado Postal 1149, Managua, Nicaragua , Tel: (505) 266-6772, Fax: (505) 266-5636, iniser@iniser.gob.ni, is the main insurance company which is owned and operated by the Government of Nicaragua. You may contact their offices in Granada at Tel: (505) 552-2780, Fax: 552-3939, León Tel: 311-2865, Fax: 311-4293, Estelí Tel: 713-2730, Fax: 713-3560 and Matgalpa Tel: 612-2904, Fax: 612-2345.

In Granada **Prisma Corredores de Seguros** Tel: (505) 552-7162, Fax: (505) 552-7157 also sells all types of insurance policies.

INISER offers a type of medical insurance with worldwide coverage called **Plan MEDISER**. Pre natal care, Surgery, hospitalization, out-patient surgery, emergency transportation, and other benfits are included in the basic policy. Additional coverage may be purchased. All residents of Nicaragua are eligible as well as their family members.

Other types of insurance offered by insurance companies are: health, life, automobile, fire, earthquake, flood, robbery, home, family insurance, insurance for students, civil responsibility, aviation, transportation of goods, bonds for bidding contracts, etc. We have been told by fellow expats that is costs about $80 yearly to insure your car against everything. Likewise they tell us it is easy to insure a house. Nicaraguan insurance companies usually settle claims quickly.

You will be pleased to know that you can buy into the Social Security health system for about $25 monthly. If you need to go to the emergency hospital there is no charge for minor treatment.

Seguros America, **Seguros Centroamericanos**, **Seguros Metropolitana**, and **Seguros Pacífico** are all majority owned by local private banks. They mainly act as reinsurers for international insurance companies. There are no foreign companies operating in Nicaragua.

Recently the Nicaraguan National Assembly passed a new law outlining the responsibilities of the Bank Superintendent and creation of an "Intendency" for insurance subordinate to the Bank Superintendent. The legislation includes rules to avoid irregularities, norms for capital requirements, and makes the superintendency's rulings binding.

Construction codes are the responsibility of the Managua municipalities. They are in charged of supervising and issuing construction permits.

The major barrier to the insurance industry is basically cost. After the catastrophic 1972 earthquake, many Nicaraguans learned the benefits of having insurance. However, most cannot afford to pay the cost of premiums.

MAKING MONEY IN NICARAGUA

Investing in Nicaragua

Basically Nicaragua's investment climate is excellent with an array of attractive opprtunites to lure investors. As you will see the government offers incentives and tax breaks in exchange for investing in some sectors. Another impotant factor is the country's ten years of uninterrupted political stability. President Alemán who took office in 1997, demonstrated a personal intrerst in welcoming new investment and his government has had a pro-foreign investment attitude. With the new global economy emerging the country can't really afford to be bogged down in any more political turmoil and internal strife. In addition, the trend toward an open economy and possible trade pacts with such nations as the U.S. and Mexico are an encouraging sign and conducive to investment in Nicaragua. Privatization of many state-run institutions will undoubtedly help attract foreign capital and the country's economic growth in the future. Nicaragua's improved infrastructure has also helped foster foreign investment. The country is easily accessible from all parts of the world by land, sea or air. The country has a highway network consisting of 1,111 miles of paved highways and 1,524 miles of other paved roads. Although some highways lack adequate maintenance. The country also has six seaports.

Phone, Internet, telex and telegraph systems link Nicaragua to the rest of the world. Nicaragua's communication system is presently being updated with the installation of fiber optic technology. Hotels and rental properties are available for businessmen.

The availity of cheap labor is another reason to invest in Nicaragua. The country's labor force of 1.7 million workers is rural-based and largely unskilled. Forty-three percent of the employed population works in agriculture, 15 percent in the manufacturing sector and 45 percent in the service sector. Since the unemployment rate has been high, there are a large number of inexperienced workers available. There is a shortage of skilled technicians and managerial personnel, although this is improving as members of the business and professional classes return from exile.

Since 1991, Nicaragua has made significant progress in opening to foreign investment. This opening has paid off in one of the fastest real GDP growth rates in Central America, and visible signs of investment and economic progress.

Nicaragua is beginning to open up to private investment in other traditionally state-run sectors. However, the national telecommunications grid is run exclusively by the state telephone company.

The foreign Investment Law guarantees the right to remit 100 percent of profits through official exchange market and repatriation of original capital three years after the inital investments. The law allows for 100% foreign ownership in all sectiors of the economy. To enjoy those guarantees, investments must be approved by the Foreign Investment Committeeof the Ministry of Development, Industry and

MAKING MONEY IN NICARAGUA

COMMON BUSINESS LINGO

A pagos	Payments, buy on time
Abogado, Licenciado	Lawyer
Acciones	Stocks
Accionista	Stockholder, Shareholder
Activo	Asset
Agrimensor	Surveyor
Al contado	For cash
Anualidad	Annuity
Año Fiscal	Fiscal year
Anticipo, prima, depósito	Down payment
Arrendamiento	Lease
Autenticar	Notarize
Avalúo	Appraisal
Certificado de depósito	C.D.s.
Cheque	Check
Cláusula	Clause
Comprador	Buyer
Contrato	Contract
Corredor	Stockbroker, real estate broker
Costo	Cost
Cuenta	Bank account
Cuenta Corriente	Checking account
Déficit	In the red, deficit
Depreciación	Depreciation
Deuda	Debt
Divisas	Foreign exchange (hard currency)
El Justo Valor del Mercado	Fair market value
Embargar, Enganchar	Attach assets
En efectivo	Pay in cash
Escritura	Deed
Estado de Cuenta	Bank statment, statement
Facilidades de Pago	Payment plan
Fideicomiso	Trust

Fidecomisario	Trustee
Financiamiento	Financing
Gastos	Costs, expenses
Giro	Money order
Hipoteca	Mortgage
Impuestos	Taxes
Intereses	Interest
Impuestos Prediales	Property taxes
Inversiones	Investments
Lote	Lot
Montar, Poner Un Negocio	Start a business
Negocios	Businesses
Notario	Notary
Pagaré	Promisory note
Parcela	Parcel of land
Plazo	Term, period of time
Precio	Price
Préstamo	Loan
Principal	Principal
Propiedad	Property
Registro	Record of ownership
Renta	Income
Rentabilidad	Profitability
Saldo	Balance of an account
Seguros	Insurance
Socio	Partner
Sociedad	Corporation
Subcontratar	To subcontract, farm out
Superávit	In the black, surplus of capital
Tasa de interés	Interest
Testaferro	Person who lends a name to a business
Terreno	Land
Traspaso	Transfer
Timbres Fiscales	Tax stamps
Valor	Value
Vendedor	Seller

MAKING MONEY IN NICARAGUA

Trade. However, most foreign investors do not seek Ministry approval because the banks freelyrepatriate profits. While in the past, Ministry approvals took over a year, recent approvals have been completed in as little as three months.

With incentives like these and the other advantages mentioned above it is no wonder many big companies have chosen to invest in Nicaragua over the last decade. Because of the country's favorable investment climate, foreign investment has increased notably. Private investment has principally gone into construction, agriculture, industry mining and tourism. Some of the major investors are: Esso Standard Oil, Bell South, the Spanish hotel group Barceló, Pepsi-Cola, Cinemark, Beyer Chemicals and Holiday Inn.

The fast-food market is booming with millions of dollars being invested in these business. According to the Ministry of Tourism, investment in the fast food industry has been successful during the last ten years. The first McDonalds in Nicaragua since it left over a decade ago reopened in July of 1998 and a TGI Fridays opened recently. There are currently 22 franchise companies operating in Nicarauga including Domino Pizza, Subway, Pizza Hut, Pollo Campero (Costa Rican franchise), Pops Ice cream (Costa Rican franchise). Quizno's Submarine Sandwiches is currently interviewing potential franchisees.

The fast food sector should continue to expand with the growth of Nicaragua's economy and middle class. Nicargaun youth begin partying at an early age and this has created a demand for many different kinds of entertainment. Couple all of this with many Nicaraguans who have lived outside of Nicaragua and acquired a taste for entertainment, fast food restaurants and other services the country doesn't provide and you can see the potential of the market.

Most impotant, many opportunities await foreigners who start new, small businesses on a shoestring, which were previously nonexistant in Nicargua. You don't have to be a big corporation to go into business. You can easily operate an Internet-based business from Nicaragua in this age of the Global Economy. Please see the start-up business ideas listed in this chapter.

Before investing or starting a business, you should take the time to do your homework. Under no circumstances should you invest right off the plane, that is to say, on your first trip to Nicaragua. Unscrupulous individuals and scamsters will always prey on impulsive buyers anywhere in the world. Be wary of any salesmen who try to pressure you into investing. Remember it's hard to start a business in your own home country. Don't imagine it will be any easier in Nicaragua where both language and customs are different.

We also suggest you ask a lot of questions and get information and assistance from any of the organizations listed below in order to thoroughly understand the business climate of the country. However, don't solely depend on the help of these organizations. You'll have to garner a lot of information and learn on your own by some trial and error. This way you can find out what works best for your particular situation

For additonal information about investments contact:

American Embassy Managua Economic and Commercial Section: e-mail amembmga@tmx.com.ni; phone 011-505-266-2291; fax 011-505-266-9056; web site http://www.usia.gov/abtusia/posts/nul/wwwhcom.html.

Nicaraguan-American Chamber of Commerce (English-speaking contact is Executive Director Desiree Pereira): e-mail amcham@ns.tmx.com.ni; phone 011-505-267-3099; fax 505-267-3098; web site at http://www.sgc.com.ni/amcham.

Nicaraguan Center for Exports and Investment (English-speaking contact is General Manager Maria Hurtado de Vijil): e-mail cei@ibw.com.ni; phone 011-505-278-3075; fax 505-278-

3129; web site at http://www.cei.org.ni.

RELOCATION, INVESTMENT and RETIREMENT CONSULTANTS is a firm we highly recommend to any newcomer or potential investor. They have many years of experience helping people in Central America, will stear you in the right direction and save you a lot of headaches and money. Their expertise, network of reliable contacts and insider information have already helped hundreds of people find success, prosperity and happiness in Costa Rica. You may contact them at: **www.liveinnicaragua.com**, **wwwliveincostarica.com** or e-mail: crbooks@racsa.co.cr.

The Tourism Boom

The number of tourists to Nicaragua has been increasing at double-digit rates, and the length of their stays has increased steadily since stability was achieved in 1990. The Nicaraguan government is expecting great growth and potential in this sector from investment in Pacific beach resorts, and ecotourism around Lake Nicaragua. According to the Institute of Tourism, tourism has been Nicaragua's third most important source of foreign exchange in the last couple of years, representing a $90 million market - an increase of 12.5 percent over 1997. Tourist arrivals grew by 10 percent in 1999, to about 416,5000 (15 percent of these from the U.S.). The Nicaraguan government expects 521,000 visitors by the year 2002 (20 percent from the U.S.). At this rate, tourism will represent Nicaragua's number two foreign exchange earner after coffee.

In 1999 President Alemán signed the Tourism Industry Incentive law to stimulate this industry. This new tax law provides tax breaks for investments in air transportation, water transportation the hospitality and lodging industry, food, beverage and entertainment service, tourism infrastructure, the arts and crafts facilities, and many more tourism related activities. To qualify for the benefits offered under the law, the investor must invest a mininum of $30,000 to $500,000, depending on the activity. Benefits, which are usually for ten years, include property and income tax ememptions, and full or partial import tax or value-added tax exemptions. Renowed names in the tourist industry such as Hampton Inn, Holiday Inn, Inter-Continental Hotels, just to name a few, are investing in Nicaragua. We have provided a copy of this list below. For more information, see the government Tourism Institute's website at **www.intur.gov.ni**.

Opportunities

Good opportunities exist for entrepreneurs who are willing to make a long-term investment in Nicaragua's emerging tourism industry. The Ministry of Tourism believes that the best opportunities over the next few years will be for projects involving Pacific beach resorts (Montelimar to San Juan del Sur) and ecotourism in the Lake Nicaragua basin (Ometepe island, Solentiname Islands, San Juan river). In addition, once Managua's three new hotels are opened, they should generate opportunities for related businesses (tour operators, restaurants, transportation, etc).

More information may be obtained from:

American Embassy Managua Economic and Commercial Section (Economic Officer JohnNaland): e-mail: usbusiness@amemb.org.ni; phone 011-505-266-2291; fax 011-505-266-9056; web site http://www.usia.gov/abtusia/posts/nu1/wwwhcom.html.

Nicaraguan Ministry of Tourism (English-speaking contact is Vice Minister Roberto Fuentes): e-mail: vero@ibw.com.ni; phone 011-505-222-6631; web site http://www.mitur.gov.ni.

Minor Obstacles to Doing Business

Nicaragua remains a poor, underdeveloped nation with

a history of political turbulence. This raises a number of obstacles for investors seeking to profit from Nicaragua's expanding tourism industry.

Poor infrastructure: although numerous road building projects are underway (many financed by foreign donors), investors wishing to take advantage of beautiful remote beaches and outlying ecotourism destinations are usually hindered by a lack of roads. Poor roads increase wear and tear on vehicles, limit tourist itineraries, and impose increased costs. There are also few hotels outside of Managua that meet international tourist standards. However, as tourism increases there will be more hotels built in outlying areas.

Political stability: despite having lost nationwide elections in 1990 and 1996 and ten years of uninterrupted democracy, the Sandinistas have so far had difficulty adapting to the role of a democratic opposition party but pose no real danger to the achievements of the last ten years.

Property rights: the Government's slow resolution of claims on thousands of properties confiscated during the Sandinista era damages the investment climate. In a recent case, a land ownership dispute forced Italian investors to put plans on hold for a 1,200 acre beach resort. Accordingly, prudent investors must consult a local attorney to carefully verify property titlebefore purchasing land.

High costs: although this should change as competition increases over the next few years, some international airfares to Managua and and upper end hotel room rates can be high. In addition, high taxes make gasoline expensive.

Service workers: in contrast to countries such as Costa Rica, workers in the Nicaraguan tourism industry typically lack training, experience, and English (or other foreign language) proficiency.

Limited promotion: unlike Costa Rica and Guatemala, the Nicaraguan government allocates little money for promoting the tourism sector. It does, however, offer a ten year tax exemption for investments in new hotels and has a draft law pending in the National Assembly that would offer additional benefits for investors in the tourism industry.

It must be pointed that the Nicaraguan Tourism Institute was very cooperative and bent over backwards" to provide a lot of assitance and materials for this book.

In spite of progress against it, corruption continues to be a factor in Nicaragua. The Aleman government has made efforts to strengthen the rule of law includingthe creation of the National Commission on Integrity and Transparency under the Vice President's direction. The government also supports efforts by the Supreme Court to strengthen the judicial system, in part by weeding out corrupt and incompetent judges. Bribery is illegal in Nicaragua but, nevertheless, does exist.

A few foreign investors have occasionally reported instances of government officials refusing to perform routine services unless bribes are paid. Additionally, the concept of "conflict of interest" is not widely understood, andpolitical factors can affect business decision-making.

The Tourist Board invites all investors to become familiar with the great advantages and benefits of the Law. **The Law 306** is intended to promote the tourist activities under a policy of sustainable development, respect and protection of the enviromentand cultural heritage. INTUR and some other state organizations are in charge of coordinating and implementing this law. The investor will get benefits as: Promotion, Certification, Fiscal Credits,Fiscal Exemptions and Concession of public lands to private investors.

A. Eligibility

The Natural and Juridic persons are covered by the benefits.

-Individuals and Companies dedicated to Tourist Activities and related activities.

-Individuals and companies participating on financing

tourist activities through loans and/or investments.

B. Activities

Tourist Activities and related businesses covered by the law are classified as follows:

1) Hotel Service Industry (Hotels, Motels, Apart hotels, Condo-hotels).
2) Investments in Protected Areas of Tourism and Ecological interest, without affecting the environment, with prior authorization from the pertinent authority (MARENA), as well as in public places of tourism andcultural interest; jointly with historical preservation.
3) Air Transportation.
4) Water Transportation (Maritime, Fluvial and Lake Transportation).
5) Internal and Ground Tourism Transportation.
6) Foods, Drinks and Amusement Services.
7) Investment in filming of motion pictures; and in events beneficial for tourism.
8) Rental of ground and water vehicles to tourists.
9) Investments in Tourism Infrastructure and connected Tourism Equipment.
10) Development of Nicaraguan Crafts; Traditional Industries; Production of Traditional Folk Musical Events and of Folk Dances; and publications and materials for Tourism promotion.
11) Small, medium and mini corporations that operate in the Tourism sector, in all areas of the sector.

C. Projects Location

The projects may be developed anywhere into the Nicaraguan territory. There are also the ZEPDT(Special Zones of Tourism Planningand Development) where the investor may get further benefits such as special financial mechanisms and maximun fiscal exemptions.

D. Minimun Investment Value (U.S. Dollars)Hotel Service Industry

	Managua Urban Zone	Outside Managua
Hotel and similar services with 15 rooms or more.	$500.000	$150.000
Paradores	$200.000	$80.000
Minimal Hostelries	$100.000	$50.000
Camping Areas	$100.000	$100.000
Foods, Drinks and Amusement Services	$100.000	$30.000
Tourist infrastructure and related equipement	$250.000	$100.000
Nicaraguan Crafts Shops	$50.000	$50.000

The activities not listed do not have minimum 1investment value but are subject to INTUR analysis and approval.

E. Benefits

For the operators or developers of tourist activities
Fiscal Exemptions
- From import fees and/or taxes (IGV or Value Added Tax)
- From taxes on Real Estate (I.B.I.)
- From Income Tax (I.R.)

Certification, Promotion and Marketing
- Paradores de Nicaragua
- Mesones de Nicaragua

State Concessions
- Tourist areas and facilities under State property

A full detailed version of this law may be accessed at www.intur.gov.ni.

Nicaragua's Nascent Stock Market

In the early 1990's the Chamorro government wanted to privatize and liberalize the economy. So, they decided to create a stock market where business could grow with more people participating in the economy. Trading opened on the Nicaraguan stock market on January 31, 1994 with a volume totaling $350 million.

Like the banking system the Nicaraguan stock market is regulated by the **Superintendencia de Bancos** (Superintendency of Banks). Eleven banks own the **Bolsa de Valores** (stock market) and various brokerage houses operate in it. Unlike the New York Stock Exchange, company shares are not bought and sold on the Nicaraguan Stock Exchange. Shares of private companies may be sold, but no companies have done so yet. Securities traded on the Bolsa are bonds. These bonds may be traded in four different markets. Some of the bonds are issued by financial institutions and other large companies seeking to expand and make investments with the capital obtained from the sale of the bonds.

A bond in Nicaragua is a sort of promisary note issued by the government, a private company or financial institution, which has a definite period for maturity and a fixed rate of interest. For instance, one can be a 15-year government bond with an interest rate of 10%. Each year the bond compounds at 10% and at the end of 15 years, the buyer may convert it into cash.

Speculating and competition in Nicaragua's stock market is not like it is in the international markets, thus making it less attractive than those markets which deal enormous amounts of money, making it possible to earn large profits.For additional information about the country's National Stock Exchange, contact: **Bolsa de Valores de Nicaragua, S.A.** Tel: (505) 278-3830, Fax: (505) 278-3836.

Courtesy of Central America Weekly.

Real Estate Investments
Rentals

Most of these upper-end rental homes have all the amenities of home: large bedrooms, views, sometimes pools , gardens with fruit trees, bathrooms with hot water, kitchens, dining rooms, a laundry room and even maid's quarters, since help is so inexpensive in Nicaragua.

Most affordable houses are unfurnished. You may find furnished homes in Nicaragua. Most cheaper places will not have hot water or the other features. When looking for a place, remember to check the phone, the shower, the closet size, kitchen cabinets, electrical outlets, light fixtures, the toilet, faucets and water pressure, locks, general security of building, windows and the condition of the stove, refrigerator and furniture, if furnished.

Also, check for traffic noise, signs of insects and rodents and what the neighbors are like. Ask about the proximity of buses and availability of taxis. Have anything you sign translated into English before you sign it. **Don't sign anything you don't understand based on the landlord's word of honor**.

As we mention later on, before deciding to live in Nicaragua permanently, it is a good idea to rent a place first or find a real estate agent who can show you around and guide you through the buying process. As you have just seen there are a variety of rental options. However, for gringos, prices sometimes may be higher. If you speak Spanish you may be able to find a better deal.

When reading the ads in the Spanish newspapers you should be familiar with the following words: *Se Alquila*-for rent, *agua caliente*-hot water, *alfombrado*-carpeted, *amueblado*-furnished, *sin muebles*-unfurnished, *baño*-bathroom, *cocina*-kitchen, *cochera* or *garaje*-garage, *contrato*-contract, *depósito*-deposit, *dormitorio*-bedroom, *guarda*-guard, *jardín*-garden, *seguro*-safe, *patio*-patio, *parqueo*-parking, *verjas*-bars, *zona verde*-grassy area, *córdobas* (Nicaraguan money).

Rental space for commercial use is available in Nicaragua. Rates vary widely depending on location, age of buildings, telecommunications availabliity, parking space and quality of security services.

As of March 2000 in Managua there are some nine commercial office centers whose rents vary from 14 to 20 dollars per square meter. There were also about 20 neighborhood shopping centers whose rates range from 5 to 12 dollars per square meter.

In Managua the are several commercial areas whose buildings were originally residential homes. These houses rates vary from 500 to 2,500 dollars per month and range from 100 to 1000 square meters in size. Buildings might lack parking space, telephone connections and/or security. Outside the capital, rental rates vary and tend to be much lower than those mentioned above. In places like Granada old homes are used as offices. In most cases this is done to take advantage of available space and save the expense of building anew structure. Also, many of the esisting buildings are colonial and can't be demolished by law.

General Advice When Buying Real Estate in Central America

If you can't afford to buy a house in the U.S. or Canada, prices of decent homes in Nicaragua are very affordable.

The value of beach property is bouind to skyrocket in the future as the country becomes more popular and developed. Many people want to realize their dream of owning a piece of paradise. For your information, beach front property is being bought-up fast, and the price of this and other prime real estate is increasing as the country becomes more popular.

Before you move to the beach, you should know that the novelty of living at the beach wears off fast. Visiting the beach for a few days or weeks is very different from living there full-time. The humidity, boredom, lack of emergency medical facilities and the general inconveniences of living in an often out-of-the-way area, are factors to consider before moving to any beach area.

Besides homes and beach property there are also farms, lots

A fixer-upper in a prime Granada location

and ranches for sale at reasonable prices, depending on their location.

When looking for property, be sure to check the comparative land values in your area to see if you are getting a good deal, and that roads, electricity and telephone service are available if you are thinking of living in a remote area. If you can't live on your property year-round, then you will have to hire a guard, caretaker or a reliable housesitter to watch it for you. Make sure boundary fences and limit signs are well maintained and visible. If you have to be an absentee owner, you can also have a friend or attorney stop by to check your property periodically.

Never **hire the same lawyer used by the seller of the property**. Also, don't forget to check that you are buying the land from its rightful owner. Some owners have sold their land to several buyers. You can protect your real estate investment further if you talk with neighbors about water shortages, safety and burglaries in the area.

Remember, always see the property in person and never buy sight unseen. Don't forget to see if you need special permits to build. Be sure to check the comparative land values in your area to see if you are getting a good deal, and that roads, electricity and telephone service are available if you are thinking of living in a remote area.

We suggest that in some cases you rent for at least six months. However, whether to rent or buy first really depends on your comfort level. Make sure to buy where it's easy to rent or sell your home in case you change your plans or in the event of a personal emergency.

To find a house or land to purchase look for a well-recommended realtor who can identify true market value like the real estate agencies we list in this section. You may also want to see the listings in th is book   Also, look around; go door-to-door in areas you like; and talk to other expats. Be sure to remember that the farther away you live from cities the more you get for your money.

To get a good buy you should study the market. Don't depend so much on the newspaper or hearsay. Talk to as many people as you can. Nothing works better that word of mouth for finding good deals. Practice your negotiating skills. You may be better off having a trustworthy bilingual Nicaraguan search for you and do your negotiating. Your realtor or lawyer should also be able to assist you.

Building A Home

In Nicaragua you can build your dream house, if you so desire, since land, labor and materials are inexpensive. One North American we know built a beautiful beach home. However, think twice about undertaking such a project because you could be flirting with disaster. Many foreigners who have built homes complain that it sounds easier than it really is. Be sure to talk with foreigners who have built homes to see what obstacles they encountered.

An American is restoring this colonial home in Granada.

Nicaragua, S.A.

For the savvy investor who goes the extra mile, we would like the opportunity to take you there.

Professional real estate services for the sophisticated investor or the informed optimist who appreciates real value.

The Real Estate Leaders
sm

E-mail: remax@tmx.com.ni
Ph: (505) 552-3009
Fax: (505) 552-2584
Website: www.remax.com

Nobody sells more Real Estate than REMAX!

Invest In

The Last Frontier

www.NicaraguanLand.com

If you do decide to build a home on your land, there are several steps required. First, conduct a preliminary study, which should be completed before you buy the land. Also, be sure to see if your lot has access to water, drainage, electricty and telephone services.

Speculating

If you are interested in purchasing real estate for investment purposes, you will be pleased to know that the government welcomes your investment.

Before buying a home or making any other real estate investment, we suggest you educate yourself by studying the Nicaraguan real estate market. A few gringos we encountered are restoring old homes in the Granada area. This seems to be a good long-term investment.

Rules For Buying Property in Nicaragua

Nicaragua has made impressive progress in recent years in consolidating democratic institutions and fostering economic growth. The country's GDP grew by 5 percent in 1997, its best performance since 1981. For 1999, the goal of 6 percent GDP appears within reach.

Construction, real estate and tourism are among the fastest growing sectors, but land prices are still low by U.S. standards and good investment opportunities still exist. However, due to still-unresolved cases stemming from confiscations of private property under the Sandinistaregime in the 1980s, buying land in Nicaragua must be done with care.

Steps To Buying and Registering Land:

To buy property in Nicaragua, you can either do most of the work yourself or hire local specialists to do much of the leg work. When hiring local specialists, it is important to agree atthe outset on a fixed fee for their services

A. Identify the property of your choice, usually by the recommendation of a friend or a local real estate agent (who earns a negotiable commission, usually between 5 and 10 percent). Be wary of property whose ownership changed hands during the 1980s.

B. At this point, you may either hire a local attorney or proceed on your own to ask the seller for a copy of the property's title (*escritura de propiedad*), evidence that it has no liens on it (*libertad de gravamen*), and its "*certificado catastral.*" Often, owners are hesitant to provide copies of titles. In such cases, you may ask the seller for the information shown on the title (propertynumber, volume number, page number, entry number) or for a copy of the property's registration (*certificado registral*) showing the last three owners (*lo últimos tres asientos*) and the absence of liens.

C. Next, have a lawyer review the documentation (*escritura de propiedad*, *certificado registral*, and *libertad de gravamen*) to verify that the property's seller has clear title.

D. After you have verified the land has no liens, a notary can prepare a sales agreement.

E. After the transaction, you or your attorney may then register the property in the *Registro Publico de la Propiedad Inmueble*. To be considered the legal owner of the property, you should possess the property title properly annotated by the registrar.

Real Estate Taxes

Real estate taxes are 1% of value of the property and are paid to the Municipal Government. Farm land of up to 30 manzanas (42.6 hectares) is exempted from real estate taxes.

Insurance

Local firms offer coverage for fire, earthquake and floods but not acts of war.

Special Considerations for Tourism Projects

Chapter IX of the May 1997 Tax Reform Law authorizes special benefits for tourism projects for those who invest 200,000 cordobas in the Departments of Carazo, Granada or Rivas, or 300,000 *córdobas* on the Atlantic Coast. Those benefits are import tax exemption and luxurytax exemption (for construction materials, etc.). However, if the business fails or is converted to another business you must pay luxury taxes.

Special Considerations for Foreign Investors

Foreign Investors may, but are not required, to register investments and negotiate a foreign investment agreement with the Ministry of Economy and Development. This guarantees the investor the following privileges under Foreign Investment Law:

1. Repatriation of foreign capital, less any losses incurred, 3 years after the capital to be repatriated entered the country.
2. Remittance abroad of the net profits generated by the capital registered.
3. Prompt, adequate and effective compensation in the case of expropriation for reasons of public utility and social interest.

In addition to the benefits listed above, other tax benefits may be individually negotiated depending on the type of business incorporated. Investors who do not register their capital maystill make remittances through the parallel market, although these transactions are not guaranteedby law. The U.S. Embassy is aware of no investor who has encountered remittance difficulties since the inception of the Foreign Investment Law

Prominent Nicaraguan Real Estate Firms:
Bienes Raíces Alpha, S.A.
Las Palmas detrás del TELCOR, Managua
TELEFAX: 505-266-5678

Bienes Raíces Sotelo & Novoa, S.A.
Cine Altamira, 2 1/2c. abajo, #437, Managua
TEL: 505-277-3401; FAX: 505-278-2790

Blandón Bienes Raíces
Sandy's Carretera a Masaya, 2c. arriba, #76, Managua
TEL: 505-278-5306; FAX: 505-278-0045

Global Real Estate
Esperanza Vallecillo, President
Rotonda Rubén Darío, 1c. Sur, 20 vrs. Oeste, Managua
Tel/Fax: 278-2108, 270-2413
E-mail: global@ibw.com.ni

González Pasos Bienes Raíces
Parque Las Palmas, 1/2c. al oeste, Managua
Apartado Postal 2130, Managua
Tel: 505-266-8910; Fax: 505-266-1002
E-mail: gonpasos@ibw.com.ni Internet:
www.GonzalezPasosRealtors.com/

Rappaccioli International Investment, S.A.
Tel/fax: 305-665-2187 (Miami), 505-266-6763

Perkoff Real Estate
106 St. Lucía, Granada
Tel: 505-552-7488 Fax: 505-552-2776 Cel: 505-776-6483
E-mail: perkoff@ibw.com.ni

Real Team Bienes Raíces, S.A.
Sandy's Carretera a Masaya, 2c. arriba, 20 vrs. al lago,
Managua. Tel: 505-278-2676 Fax: 505-278-2657

RE/MAX Nicaragua
David Smith
Calle El Arsenal, #305, Granada
TEL: 505-552-3009; FAX: 505-552-2584
E-mail: remax@tmx.com.ni
www.remax.com

MAKING MONEY IN NICARAGUA

Sniders Realty
P.O. Box 3931, Managua
TEL: 505-278-3230; TELFAX: 505-552-4702
E-mail: srealty@ibw.com.ni Internet: www.ibw.com.ni/~srealty/

Tierra Nica
Contact Charlie Southwell
Tel/Fax: 505-552-3199 Cel: 088-52489
E-mail:Tierranica@yahoo.com,
www:nicaraguaproperty.com

Finding Work

Foreigners can only work when they are legal residents. However, you may still invest in the country and employ Nicaraguans.

We have some discouraging news for those living on small pensions and hoping to supplement their income with a part or full-time job or for others who need to work just to keep busy. Finding work can be very difficult but not impossible. In the first place, it is not easy for a Nicaraguan not to mention foreigners who don't speak fluent Spanish, to find permanent work. To make matters worse the employment rate is very high which makes finding a job very difficult.

If you are one of the few foreigners who has mastered Spanish, you may be able find work in tourism or some other related field. However, your best bet may be to find employment with a North American firm doing business in Nicaragua. The best-paying jobs are with multinational corporations. It is best to contact one of these companies before moving to Nicaragua. You may be able to find a job as a salesman, an executive or a representative, depending on your qualifications. Look for websites which have information about employment overseas

When local companies hire foreigners, they are generally looking for a solid educational background and an entrepreneurial spirit that some companies find lacking in Nicaraguans. It helps to have a degree from a well-known U.S. university—preferably an MBA.

Even if you know little or no Spanish, you have a chance of finding work as an English teacher at an American school or language school. As supplemental income or busywork, this is fine, but you won't make a living given the kind of life style you are probably accustomed to. If you can find work at a private bilingual school, you can probably earn a slightly better salary. The competition for these jobs is very stiff, preference is given to bilingual Nicaraguans, and most foreigners hang on to these coveted positions.

Eventually you will able to use one of your skills to provide some service to the growing expatriate community in Nicaragua. Everyone has a talent or speciality they can offer. For example, if you are a writer, journalist or have experience in advertising, you might try starting an English language newspaper. Unfortunately, if you are a retired professional such as a doctor or lawyer, you can't practice in Nicaragua because of certain restrictions but can offer your services as a consultant to other foreigners and retirees.

Some foreigners may try to work under-the-table. This practice is illegal and you do so at your own risk if you want to bear the consequences. If you don't seek remuneration, you can always find volunteer work to keep yourself busy. This kind of work is legal, so you don't need a work permit or run the risk of being deported for working illegally.

Starting a Business

As a foreigner, you can invest in Nicaragua and even start your own business with only some restrictions.

MAKING MONEY IN NICARAGUA

Best prospects for U.S. sales include agricultural commodities, fertilizer, farm equipment, food processing packaging machinery, medical supplies, data processing equipment, electrical equipment, franchising, construction equipment, and U.S. motor vehicles and spare parts. Best investment opportunities exist in export-oriented manufacturing, tourism, mining, and agriculture. There may also be opportunities in road building, water system construction, and electricity generation. If you plan to go into business here it is very important to be aware of the local consumer market in order to succeed. You should know where most of the country's purchasing power is located and where the majority of country's population resides. Intelligent business people will try to meet the needs of this group.

You may also think about targeting tourists, middle and upper-class Nicaraguans There is a wealth of opportunity available in tourist-related businesses. What you essentially do in tourism is target foreigners who have disposable in come to spend abroad.

Upper-class Nicaraguans also have money and the greatest purchasing power. They don't mind spending a little more on good quality products. The majority of the country's upper middle and upper-class consumer's values are now more akin to their U.S. counterparts. You can see this starting to take hold with a number of shopping malls being built in Managua. As the economy improves and the country develops middle and upper lower class Nicaraguans will want all of the goodies like cellular telephones .

One group to target is the potential foreign residents market. Once the number of foregn residents grow, all you will have to do is look for a product to fill their needs. Most will yearn for some hard -to-find-products from home and would rather buy them in Nicaragua than go to the U.S. to shop.

Nicaragua is ripe for innovative foreigners willing to take a risk and start businesses that have not previously existed. Start-up costs for small businesses are less than in the U.S. or Canada. Many of the same types of businesses which have been successful in the U.S. and Canada will work if researched correctly. There is definitely a need for these types of businesses. You just have to do your homework and explore the market. Be aware that not everything that works in the U.S. will work here. Also you may have to adapt your idea because of the vagaries of the local market and different purchasing power. Don't get any grandiose ideas since the country has only a little over 4 million people and many live in poverty. You cannot expect to market products on a large scale as in the States. Nicaragua's local artisans make scores of beautiful handcrafted products such as furniture, pottery and cloth. With so many choices, a smart person can find something to sell back home.

There will be many potential business opportunities worth

One enterprising American started a full-service laundry in Granada.

exploring: building and selling of small homes for middle class Nicaraguans or foreigners; an import-export business; desktop publishing; computer services and support; U.S. franchises; importing new foods; specialty bookstores; restaurants and bars; an auto body and paint shop; consulting; or speciality shops catering to North Americans and upperclass Nicaraguans.

Nicaraguans and other Central Americans love anything novel from America. There are many stores selling both new and used, trendy U.S.-style clothing. For example, Costa Rican teenagers dress like their counterparts in the States and even watch MTV. U.S. fast food restaurants like Taco Bell, Burger King , Pizza Hut and MacDonald's are extremely popular. Real estate speculation can be lucrative if you have the know-how and capital.

Courtesy of the U.S.Embassy in Managua.

Occasional Roadblocks to Doing Business in Nicaragua

The major roadblocks are:

(1) Unpredictability of enforcement of contracts and a cumbersome legal system. The enforcement of judicial rulings is sometimes uncertain. Although the government is working to establish clear rules applicable to all, the rules of the game aresometimes changed by sudden government decree or political considerations which can significantly disrupt business planning. Requests for bribes do occur.

(2) Slow resolution of Sandinista-era property claims (including U.S. citizen properties). Potential investors should consult a local attorney to verify property titles before purchasing property.

(3)Sometimes high operating costs in terms of transportation,

Start Up Business Ideas in Nicaragua

Spanish/English language schools
An English, French, German or Italian newspaper
A private bilingual elementary or high school
Business consulting firm
New agricultural products
Internet consulting and web page design
Translating service
Bred and breakfast hotel
Restaurants
Automobile parts
State of the art gas stations
Fast food franchises
Copy centers
Importing used cars from the U.S.
Computer sales and software
Laundry (self-service)
Bicycle shop
Bakery
Money transfers
Housing renovation
Hardware store
Food imports
Toy store
Athletic footware
Private postal service
Secretarial and typing service

MAKING MONEY IN NICARAGUA

Food imports
Toy store
Athletic footware
Private postal service
Janitorial and maid service
English bookstore
Charter fishing and scuba diving
Foreign residents association
Travel agency
Super and mini markets
24-hour pharmacy with home delivery
Pizzeria
Celular phones and beepers
Office products and supplies
Offshore bank
Money changing
Furniture factory
Cigar exporting
Swimming pool construction
Real estate office and find-a-home
Satellite T.V. and cable
An English radio station
A driving school
Pawn shop
Voicemail
Manufacturing of clothing
US and European newspaper distribution

electricity, and telephone. Power outages also lead to higher costs.

(4) An incomplete intellectual property rights regime. The Aleman government signed a bilateral IPR agreement with the U.S.and is working to improve domestic legislation. New copyright legislation was passed July 5, 1999, which will greatly strengthen copyright protection once the law is published in the official government gazette. Penalties will be phased in over a12-month period. The National Assembly is considering laws to protect developers of new plant varieties and information sent by satellite and other signal carriers. The government is working on laws to protect integrated circuit designs and well-known trademarks. An updated patent law is also being reviewed before being sent to the national assembly.

(5) Arbitrary or slow bureaucracy. Doing business in Nicaragua can sometimes mean becoming involved with slow-moving government approvals. Foreign investors also complain about arbitrary customs procedures and valuations.

Courtesy of the U.S.Embassy in Managua

Common Business Sense In Nicaragua

It is important to keep in mind that running a business in Nicaragua is not like managing a business in the United States because of unusual labor laws, the Nicaraguan work ethic and the Nicaraguan way of doing business.

In order for a foreigner to own a business, a Nicaraguan corporation or *Sociedad Anónima* should be formed (see the section titled "Taxes" in the last chapter).

We also recommend that you do a thorough feasibility study. Spend at least a few months thoroughly analyzing the potential. Don't assume that what works in the U.S. will work in Nicaragua. Check out restrictions and the tax situation. And most important, choose a business in which you have a vast prior experience. It's much more difficult to familiarize yourself with a new type of business in a foreign country.

Success Stories in Nicaragua

By Christopher Howard

A Dedicated Educator

Mary Ellen Norman is the director of the American-Nicaraguan School in Granada. Mary originally came to the school over ten years ago on a short term basis. However, she fell in love with Nicaragua and her job and has never left. Under her auspices the school has flourished offering a complete accredited academic program with all subjects in English. Her school is located on a hill overlooking the city of Managua. The academic program is excllent and the school is on the American calendar. The campus is very imressive. All of the rooms have air conditioning, there is a huge gymnasium, running track and much more.

A Real Estae Genius

Sandy Perkoff came to Nicaragua about two years ago after residing in Costa Rica for over 20 years. He ran a successful car rental company and dabbled in real estate during his stint in Costa Rica. Presently lives in the colonial city of Granada with his Costa Rican wife, Lucía. He is a personable man who knows everyone in town. Sandyis a highly-skilled creative entrepreneur working in real estate. He has brokered several properties and was involved in the sale of a multimillion dollar project at the beach. His pet project is the restoration of a colonial style house in downtown Granada. He has virtually had to rebuild it from the ground up. When it is finished he will have a real gem. Sandy plans to live in the house as his primary residence. He also owns a beautiful parcel of land overloking a nearby lagoon. Knowing Sandy, he will eventually develop the lakeside property.

A Travel Business

Rob, another friend of ours from Florida has had a successful travel business based in Costa Rica and Florida for many years. He is a visionary and is well aware of the Nicaragua's impending travel boom. It is only a question of time before he dominates the travel scene in Nicaragua. At present he restoring two old homes in Granada to lodge tourists.

A One-of-a-Kind Hotel

Bill Harper came to Nicaragua from Costa Rica and wasted no time in starting a small hotel and restaurant and hotel for budget travelers. The funky Hospedaje Central is one of Granada's "in places." The food is reasonably priced and the selection is excellent. At night the place booms. You can find a interesting crowd composed of local expats, foreign travellers and other characters socializing into the wee hours of the night. What really makes the place is Bill's congenial personality. Everyone feels at home thanks to his outgoing style. He is very knowledgeable about the Granada area and will be happy answer all of your questions.

A Beautiful Place to Stay

Anita Weissman came to Graanada with her husband, Larry, and converted a beautiful colonial home int acharming hotel. The place really has to seen to believed. They have opened their home up to all of their guests. The place is beautiful and spacious with its high ceilings tasteful paint, sumptuous dining room, kitchen and a whole lot more. Larry boasts a huge collection of different brands of chile prominently displayed on the shelves of his kitchen. Larry and his wife even offer massages and manicures for their guests.

A Transplated Canadian

J.D. came to Nicaragua after living in Antigua Guatemala. Together with some of his hometown friends they restored an old home and turned it into one of the city's best watering holes. On Monday night the place fills up to watch Monday Night Footbal games from the states on a large screen T.V. The atmosphere is very comfirtable.

Laundromat Robert

Robert got his nickname because he founded the first laundromat in Granada. He is a man with a heart of gold A couple of years ago he came to Nicaragua after Hurricane Mitch had devastated the country and Robert helped rebuild a local schood with his own money. Originally he came to Nicaragua in his dune buggy. .Thus he first earned the name of "Dune Buggy" Robert. He says he doesn't make a lot from his laundroymat but is content because he provides jobs for the locals. He's not i it for the money since he is independently wealthy.

MAKING MONEY IN NICARAGUA

Remember a trustworthy partner or manager can mean the difference in success and failure. Make sure you choose a partner with local experience. Don't trust anyone until you know them and have seen them perform in the work place.

You will be doomed to failure if you intend to be an an absentee owner. We know of someone who founded an business which initially did very well. However, they moved back to the States and put a couple of employees in charge and everything eventually fell apart: sales began to lag, money went uncollected, checks began to bounce, expenses were unaccounted for and incompetent salesmen were hired. Their potentially successful business just couldn't be run from abroad.

You have to stay on top of your business affairs. At times it is hard to find reliable labor and the bureaucracy can be stifling. If you have a business with employees, be aware of your duties and reponsibilities as an employer. Know what benefits you need to pay in addition to salary to avoid problems. Remember, the more employees you have, the more headaches.

Be sure you have enough money in reserve in case of an emergency. You should have an ample reserve of capital to fall back on during the initial stage of your business in case things get rough.

Talk to people, especially the "oldtimers," who have been successful in business, and learn from them. Profit from their mistakes, experiences and wisdom. Don't rush into anything that seems too good to be true. Trust your intuition and gut feeling at times. However, the best strategy and rule of thumb is to, "Test before you invest."

During the time we have lived in Central America, we have seen many foreigners succeed and fail in business ventures. About three in ten foreigners succeed in business in Central America. There are few success stories and a lot of failures, in areas as diverse as bars, restaurants, car-painting shops, language schools, real estate, tourism, bed & breakfasts to name a few. People have impossible dreams about what business will be like in Central America. It is a gigantic mistake to assume the success will come easy in Nicaragua. Initially starting any business usually takes more time and more money. Also many unforseen problems are surley to arise.

If you decide to purchase an existing business make sure that it is not over priced. Try to find out the owner's real motives for selling it. Make sure you aren't buying a "white elephant." Ask to see the books and talk to clients if you can. To ferret out a good deal, look for someone who is desperate to sell their business. Check the newspapers and ask everyone you know if they know of someone selling a business. Finally, make sure there aren't law suits, debts, unpaid creditors or liens against the business.

After reading the above, if you still have questions or are confused, we advise you to consult a knowledgeable Nicaraguan attorney or the other sources we have listed in this book for further information. Finally, if you plan to invest or do business in a Spanish-speaking country you should definitely purchase Wiley's *English-Spanish Dictionary*, Barron's *Talking Business in Spanish*, or Passport Books *Just Enough Business Spanish*. All of these guides contain hundreds of useful business terms and phrases.

RED TAPE

Dealing With Bureaucracy in Latin America

Just as in the rest of Latin America, Nicaragua is plagued by a more inefficient bureaucratic system than is the U. S. This situation is exaggerated by the Latin American temperament, the seemingly lackadaisical attitude of most bureaucrats and the slower pace of life south of the border. The concept of time is much different from that in the U. S. or Canada. When someone says they'll do something *"ahorita"* (which literally means right now), it will take from a few minutes to a week, or maybe forever. It is not unusual to wait in lines for hours in banks and government offices and experience unnecessary delays that would seldom occur in the U. S.

This situation is very frustrating for foreigners who are used to fast, efficient service. It can be especially irritating if you don't speak good Spanish. Since very few people working in offices speak English and most North Americans speak little else, it is advisable to study basic Spanish. Above all, learn to be patient and remember that you can get the best results if you do not push or pressure people. Try having a good sense of humor and using a smile. You will be surprised at the results.

A few words of caution—there are some individuals, who pass themselves off as lawyers or who befriend you and offer to help you with red tape, claiming they can short-cut the bureaucratic system because of their contacts. As a general rule, avoid such individuals or you will lose valuable time, run the risk of acquiring forged documents, most certainly lose money and experience indescribable grief.

Since bribery and pay offs are common in most Latin American countries and government employees are underpaid, some people advise paying them extra money to speed up paper work or circumvent normal channels. This bribery is illegal and not recommended for foreigners; they can be deported for breaking the law. However, in some instances it may be necessary to pay extra money to get things done. Use your own discretion in such matters. A tip here and there for a small favor can accelerate bureaucratic delays.

Everyone planning to live, retire or do business in Nicaragua should know that the American Embassy can help with: Social Security and Veterans benefits, notarizing documents, obtaining new U. S. passports, registering births of your children and getting a U.S. visa for your spouse (if you choose to marry a Nicaraguan). They also assist in obtaining absentee ballots for U.S. elections and getting U.S. income tax forms and information. If you get into any legal trouble in Nicaragua, however do not expect help from the U.S. Embassy.

How to Become a Legal Resident of Nicaragua

People find Nicaragua attractive and want to live in the

RED TAPE

country for a myriad of reasons: warm year-round weather, the rat race and hustle-bustle in the US, a new start in life, inexpensive living and retirement, tax benefits, the country's low-cost health care system, start a business or invest, learn Spanish, separation or divorce, enjoy the country's growing expatriate community and even to find companionship, to name a few. Whatever your motives may be for wanting to move to Nicaragua, there are a number of ways to remain in the country on a long-term basis.

Tourists from North America and many countries in Europe may now remain legally in the country for three months without having to apply for permanent residency. You can get extensions on your tourist visa. You may own property, start a business or make investments with no more than a tourist visa. But opening a bank account can prove to be hard as a tourist. You most certainly need good references from someone already established in the country like a Nicaraguan or foreign

Most foreign resident have to visit the Immigration Department in Managua.

resident.

If you plan to reside in Nicaragua full-time one of Nicaragua's permanent residency programs will appeal to you. It is advantageous to obtain residency so you can take advantage of the many attractive incentives available to foreign residents.

We interviewed a couple of Noth Americans who recently obtained residency and the process basically goes like this. First, you need to get a police report from the US stating you have no criminal recond. It must be notarized and you need a letter stating that the person who notarized your report is really a notary.

Second, you'll have to go through the exact same process for your birth certificate. Third you'll also need to prove you have a fixed income of at least $400 per month (see the next section for details). For instance if you receive a social security check you may ask them for a statement of your monthhy income. This statement may be obtained from the US Embassy. Make sure the put their official seal on it or you may have problems.

Next, you'll need to make a list of what you plan to import to Nicaragaua under the $10,000 exemption you'll receive as a resident. You really are better off bringing very little and trying to buy as much as you can in Nicaragua. For example, furniture is very inexpensive. A friend of ours bought a beautiful 8-foot hand-made wood table for $80. It would have easily cost a few hundred dollars in the US. On your initial visit you should see what's available on the local market to get a good idea of what you absolutely need to import.

If you plan to import a car, try to get an inexpensive model so as to not use up all of the $10,000 exemption. You can really find affordable used cars in Nicaragua. The tax you pay is less that half of what it is in neighboring Costa Rica. You really

RED TAPE

don't need to use up a large part of your exemption by importing an expensive car. Both the availability of inexpensive cars and their affordability are compelling reasons which make Nicaragua more attractive to foreigners.

You'll need an attorney to help you with your residency. We have provided a partial list of laywers in this chapter. It is also a good idea to talk to other foreigners who have gone through the process of obtaining residency. They can usually recommend a good attorney. Lawyers usually charge from $650 to $1000 for helping you obtain your residency.

You may have to go Nicaragua's Immigration Department to take care of your immigration related business. The country's main immigration office is located in Managua. Dirección General de Migración y Extranjería Tel: (505) 244-3989 can be reached by giving a taxi driver the following directions in Spanish: " De los semáforos de la Tendrí 3 al lago or frente al Catsatro or Antigua Istalaciones de INSS." However, any lawyer you hire should do all of your legwork. If you speak Spanish you'll be pleased to know that there are lawyers, notories and photographers who have small offices directly across from the immigeation office. If you are in a jam any of these business can help you with your paper work.

El Güegüense Tel: (505) 552-4641 is an office in near the main plaza in Granada which will notarize papers, help with visa extensions and other immigration matters.

Below is the complete version of Nicaragua's Residency Law to help you understand its find points. If there are parts that are unclear to you, we suggest you consult with a Nicaraguan attorney.

RESIDENT PENSIONERS OR INDIVIDUALS LIVING ON INVESTMENTS ACT DECREE NO. 628 NATIONALCONSTITUTIONAL ASSEMBLY OF THE REPUBLIC OF NICARAGUA

Article 1. Entry into the country is authorized for persons under the category of "RESIDENT PENSIONERS" or "INDIVIDUALS LIVING ON INVESTMENTS".

Article 2. For the purpose of this Act, "RESIDENT PENSIONER" shall be understood to be any person who has received a pension or retirement from the government, from official agencies or from private enterprise, in his respective country, and "INDIVIDUAL LIVING ON INVESTMENTS" shall be any person who has a stable, permanent income generated abroad. The categories of Resident Pensioner or Individual Living on Investments, for immigration purposes, include the spouse, children and other dependents of anyone who obtains the status of Resident Pensioner or Individual Living on Investments.

Article 3. In order to obtain residency in the category mentioned in the previous article, the interested party must verify that he is more than forty-five years of age, and prove that he belongs to either of the two categories referred to in Article 1, and has stable and permanent monthly income, generated abroad, of no less than FOUR HUNDRED DOLLARS, in U.S. currency, or its equivalent in any other foreign currency, plus ONE HUNDRED DOLLARS per month for each member of his family who depends on him for subsistence in this country.

Article 4. Any Nicaraguans who have lived abroad permanently for more than TEN YEARS, and who can prove they have an income generated abroad, in accordance with the conditions stipulated in the precrding article, may obtain the benefits established in this Act. Also, any citizen of this country who has received a pension from other governments or foreign businesses, established in this country, may be included in the status of "Resident Pensioner" provided the income is generated abroad.

Article 5. Persons protected under this law will have a one time customs exemption, and exemption from other current or future import taxes, of TEN THOUSAND DOLLARS($10,000.00 U.S.) for importing their household goods. They may also apply to obtain immigration benefits for their dependents. Furthermore, they shall have an exemption from income taxes levied on income declared as earned abroad, when eligible for the rights granted under this Act.

In case they transfer the property mentioned in this article, within three years after entering this country, they must pay the taxes from which they were exempted.

Artice 6. Beneficiaries may also import an automobile for personal or general use, free from import taxes, customs duty, sales taxes and financial stability taxes. Any vehicle so brought into this country may be sold, assigned or transferred to another person, exempt from said taxes after five years have elapsed from the time it was imported.

Once the previously mentioned period has elapsed, the beneficiary is automatically given the right to import another vehicle, and so forth, successively, every five years.

In the event that a vehicle is lost due to theft or total loss due to fire, a collision or an accident ocurring in any five year period, beneficiaries may acquire another vehicle, without being subject to said taxes.

In either case, the corresponding amount shall not be taken into account for the exemption established in the previous article.

Article 7. If the benficiary waives his status as "Resident Pensioner" or "IndividualLiving on Investments", within the time periods indicated in Article 5 and 6, he must pay any taxes he was exempted from.

Article 8. Any person who enters the country as "ResidentPensioners" or "individuals Living on Investments", in compliance with the requirements established in this Act, may remain in the country for an indefinite period of time; however, he may not engage in any type of industrial or commercial activity, nor hold any paid job paid by domestic funds, except for public office, as established in Article 30 Cn. Exempted from this restriction are "Resident Pensioners or "Individuals Living on Investments" who have real property in Nicaragua that has been publicly recorded, for a minimum amount of one hundred thousand dollars in foreign currency, and who make investments which generate profit for this country, according to the criteria of the Secretary of Economics, Industry and Commerece. In the case of married couples, the restriction in this article applies to both spouses.

Nicaraguan beneficiaries engaging in any of the activities contemplated in this article may not continue receiving the benefits they have been granted by this Act.

Article 9. The secretary of Economy, Industry, and Commerce, through the General Office of Tourism, shall be the agency in charge of reviewing and deciding on applications for obtaining benefits under this Act.

Article 10. All persons interested in obtaining the benefits of this Act must apply with the Secretary of Economy, Industry and Commerce at the General Office of Tourism, or with authorized Nicaraguan Consular offices abroad. They must submit the documentation which provides evidence of the conditions established in Article 2 of this Act, of their nationality, their good standing and a certificate of health, certifying that the applicant does not suffer from mental illness nor any infectious or contagious disease. The GeneralOffice of Tourism will issue a Resolution within fifteen days after the receipt of the application, and shall make to the Secretary of Foreign affairs, at the Department of Imigration in order to issue the Residency Identification for a " Resident Pensioner" or "Individual Living on Investments".

Once the application has been accepted, the Secretary of Economy, Industry and Commerce, through the general office of Tourism, will officially notify the Secretary of the Treasury and Public Credit and the General Customs Office, will recommend that the exemptions and dispensation from import duties be granted to the applicant.

Article 11. All interested parties may process their applications, in the country where they reside, with the authorized Nicaraguan consul officials, in compliance with the provisions established herein.

Once the process has been completed, said official shall send the respective file to the Secretary of Economy, Industry and Commerce, for its review and decision. The results shall be reported to the entity which sent said file.

Article 12. All applications must be filed on paper with a seal for fifty cents of a Códova, and the signature of the certificate shall be duly certified by a Notary or official in the Foreign Service, in keeping with the previous article, and shall provide the following documents:

a). Certificate of the pension, retirement or income stated on the application, issued by the respective agencies, expressly stating the monthly amount, and that it is permanent, and state any condition it is subject to.

When the party issuing said certificate is a private entity with an unknown or dubious financial solvency, there must be also a certificate from a Certified Public Accountant attesting that, after a review of the accouting records of the private entity in question, he can sign that said entitiy is in the financial position to pay out the corresponding pension or income, for a minimum of five years.

b) A certificate of nationality or passport from the applicant and his dependents.

c). A passport or a valid travel document in order to provide proper evidence of his status as a foreigner.

d). A certified issued by an entity such as The National Registry or Hall of Records, from the place where he has resided for the last six months, regarding the personal record of the applicant and spouse. This certification may be substituted, in proper cases, according to the criteria of the Secretary of Economy, Industry and Commerece, the General Office of Tourism, by a sworn statement from three Nicaraguan nationals, with recognized standing, who attest that they know the applicant, and guarantee that he has been a person of good conduct in the past.

e.) A list of items to be imported by the interested party.

Two copies of all documents must be submitted. passports must must be issued along with two photocopies. The Office of the General Division of Tourism handling the processing of applications, shall immediately proceed to compare the acompanying photocopies to see whether they correspond to the original, and, if so, shall return the passport to the interested party in the same process.

Article 13. Probative documents which must be submitted, in accordance with this Act, must be issued in compliance with the legal requirements, provided for in the respective legislation, and written in the Spanish language.

Any document in foreign languages must be translated into Spanish in a legal manner. For such documents to be valid in Nicaragua, it is essential for them to be properly authenticated.

Article 14. If the documents or reports provided for granting the benefits offered by this act prove to be false, sanctions shall be applied ordering immediate payment of the exempted taxes plus 10% fine, and the credential issued by the pertinent agencies will be cancelled, in accordance with this act.

Article 15. Foreigners entering the country with the status of "Resident Pensioner" or "Individual Living on Investments", for industrial purposes, involving an amount of no less than one hundred thousand dollars, may receive the benefits provided on Article 19, paragraph 1) of the Political Contitution.

Article 16. This act repeals any other previous provisions which are inconsistent with it, and will go into effect upon its publication in La Gaceta, the Official Reporter.

REQUIRED DOCUMENTS AND INFORMATION FOR PROCESSING APPLICATIONS FOR RESIDNET PENSIONERS OR RESIDENTS LIVING ON INVESTMENTS

1. An application, in writing, on paper, with the legal seal, duly authenticated by a notary public.

2. Documents authenticating a stable and permanent monthly income, generated abroad, of no less than U.S. $400.00 (FOUR HUNDRED DOLLARS), plus U.S. $100.00 (ONE HUNDRED DOLLARS) for each member of the family who depends on applicant.

3. Birth certificatc(s).

4. A photocopy of the applicant's and dependent's passports.

5. A certificate of good conduct or criminal record (police report), issued by the compentant office, from the place where he has lived for the last six (6) months.

6. A health certificate.

7. A description of household goods.

8. Specifications of the automobile to be imported.

9. All documents must be accompanied by two (2) copies, be translated into Spanish, and be duly certified and filed with the General Secretary of the Secretary of Tourism.

Courtesy of the Nicaraguan Institute of Tourism

Immigration and Other Matters
Basic Requirements

All visitors entering Nicaragua must have a passport that will be valid for at least six months after entering the country. Citizens of most countries may enter with only a passport and the required purchase of a $5 tourist card at the point of entry. U.S. citizens do not need to obtain a visa for visits less than 90 days. However, initially U.S. citizens can only stay 30 days but are allowed two 30-day estentions. Visa requirements have been abolished for everyone from North, Central and South America, and western Europe. Citizens of other countries require a visa or tourist card.

Visas are required for stays of 90 days or more. Individuals wishing to establish themselves in the country must request a resident visa from the **Dirección General de Migración y Extranjería** (The Office of Immigration) in Managua, Tel: (505)244-3989 They are open Monday through Friday from 8am to noon and 2 to 4pm.

What foreign non-residents frequently do is, leave the country for three days after their initial ninety days have expired. Many go neighboring Costa Rica. This way they can stay in the country almost indefinately as "perpetual tourists". However, there is some talk that people who go out every ninety days may have to get residency.

Foreigners who overstay the ninety period without renewing their papers shouldn't worry too much since they only have to pay a small penalty upon leaving the country.

If you are not a U.S. citizen, check with a Nicaraguan embassy or Consulate abroad to find out about specific visa requirements.

When leaving by air all non-resident Nicaraguans must pay a $25 departure tax.

Nicaraguan Citizenship

At present it is not in your best intetrest to obtian Nicaragua citizenship. Nicaragua doesn't recognize dual citizenship.

Getting Married

Getting married in Nicaraguans really quite simple. All you have to do is complete the required paperwork. You will need an authenticated copy of your birth certificate. Lawyers can marry people in Nicaragua much like a justice of the peace in the States. This type of marriage is called por civil and is usually quicker than a traditional church wedding or por la iglesia. In Nicaragua people get married either way.

If you do choose to have a lawyer marry you, you will need to have a couple of witnesses for the ceremony. Your lawyer will be able to round up a couple of people if you can't find anyone.

Shipping an Automobile or Household Goods to Nicaragua

Because import taxes on new cars can be high used cars are plentiful in Nicaragua The tax on a new car is around 20%. Most of the second hand cars are priced higher than they would be in the U.S. or Canada, so Nicaraguans tend to keep them longer and take better care of them. This makes resale value high.

Your're really better off buying a used car in Nicaragua. These prices and duties are half of what they are in neighboring Costa Rica. For example, a 1990 Toyota Land cruiser costs around $10,000 and a 1991 around $8,500. A 1990 Mitsubishi Montero runs around $8,800 and a 1996 model around $9,500. Please see the copy of the classified ads with car prices on page 115

The majority of automobiles in Nicaragua are made in Japan. So, most replacement parts are for Japanese automobiles. Spare parts for U.S. cars have to be imported, are expensive and sometimes hard to come by. Therefore, you should think twice about bringing an American car to Nicaraguaa. If you do decide to bring a car from the U.S. or Canada it is best to bring a Toyota, Nissan, Honda or some other Japanese import for the reasons just mentioned.

There are two ways to bring a car to Nicaragua—by sea or by land. If you ship your car to Nicaragua by boat, we suggest you contact **NICAMAR**, a Nicaraguan freight company in Miami (you may also use them for your household goods). A Nicaraguan shipper has the right contacts and experience to make shipping your car easier. You also need to contact **Ronald Lacayo** in Nicaragua at Tel: (505) 233-1444 or 263-2409. This method of transportation is relatively safe since your car can be insured against all possible types of damage.

We interviewed a couple from Chicago who had all of their household good shipped from the states and said the whole process took about 30 days from Miami. Everything arrived intact. The best part of the deal was that they had door-to-door-service. The shipping company delivered everything to their front door. They used Ronald Lacayo as a shipper and were very happy.

If you have all of your paperwork in order, your vehicle should not take more than a month at the most to reach Nicaragua depending on your port of embarkation. If your car is sent from Miami it may take less time to reach Nicaragua. From the West coast or New York, you can expect to pay more and wait longer.

Some expats sent their car via Puerto Limón, Costa Rica and said that they saved a little time. They then picked up their car there and drove it to Nicaragua.

You will have to make sure your shipping company sends the following documents or neither you or a customs agency can get your car out of customs: title or pink slip (*título de propiedad*), registration, copy of passport, original bill of lading (*conocimiento de embarque*) and the name of the shipping company. Also make sure your car has Canadian or U.S. plates or the whole process may be delayed.

Don't think you can fool the customs inspectors by putting

RED TAPE

Classified Car Ads from La Prensa

AUTOS USADOS CASA PELLAS, ACAHUALINCA

SUPER OFERTA

GARANTIA DE FABRICA

CHEVROLET S-10 D/CAB 4X4 1999 FULL EXTRA DIESEL PRECIO ESPECIAL U$15,500

TOYOTA CORONA 1993 FULL EXTRA GASOLINA 1.6 LT. MECANICO U$10,000

TOYOTA HILUX D/CAB 4X4 1987 DIESEL 2.4 LT PRECIO ESPECIAL U$6,500

MITSUBISHI MONTERO JEEP 1996 4X4 DIESEL PRECIO ESPECIAL U$9,500

TOYOTA TERCEL 1999 MECANICO F/INYECCION 1,500 CC SUPER OFERTA U$9,000

TOYOTA HILUX D/CAB 4X4 AIRE ACOND. DIESEL 2.8 LT SUPER OFERTA U$17,000

TOYOTA LAND CRUISER PRADO 1999 4X4 FULL EXTRA DIESEL 2.8 LT SUPER OFERTA U$26,000

VENTA 105 4X4

TOYOTA 4 RUNNER 98, NITIDA, FULL EXTRAS. TELF: 05523775.

ASTRO VAN DE LUJO, FULL EXTRA, GANGA. TEL: 7772828

DAIHATSU VELOSA, AÑO 93, COLOR BLANCO, FULL EXTRA, GASOLINA, MECANICA. BUENAS CONDICIONES. INTERESADOS PRESENTARSE A ANTOJITOS CHINO FRENTE A CINE CABRERA.

FORD '2000, D/CABINA, DIESEL 8CILINDROS, 4PUERTAS, TINA LARGA. TEL.: 276-2251, 088-73788

FORD CAMIONETA F250 King cab, diesel 8cil. año 87, full extras. US$5,500. Tel: 08837356.

GALLOPER '98, TURBODIESEL, FULL EXTRAS, PERFECTO ESTADO, UN SOLO DUEÑO. TEL: 088-46990.

ISUZU RODEO '93, Gas, Súper Ganga U$7,500. 276-2158.

ISUZU RODEO, en perfectas condiciones. Poco uso, una sola dueña. Año 92 full extras, versión americana. Por viaje lo doy en U$8,000. Verlo en Estacionamiento de Naciones Unidas. (contiguo a Xerox) ó llame al Tel. 077-88277.

ISUZU Trooper 86, turbo, diesel, roja, timón hidraulico, 4 wd, perfecto estado Tel. 08869672 de dia, 08856812 por la noche.

IZUSU TROOPER 87 hidráulico, llantas nuevas $4200 negociable. 2481780 / 08861088

ISUZU Año 86, perfecto estado, full extras. Tel. 064-22203.

ISUZU PUP. 85, diesel. $2,800. Tel. 2330677

ISUZU PUP diesel de trabajo, U$2,800. Tel: 277-1097/088-22251

ISUZU TROOPER, AÑO 86, DIESEL, 2 PUERTAS, U$5,000 NEG. COLEGIO RUBENIA 1C.ABAJO N-5 PORCHE DE TEJA, DE 6:PM A 8:PM- 088-71072

MAZDA 2000 año 88, tina larga, diesel, aire, como nueva US$5,550 USA. Tel.: 2600792, 07788827

MAZDA B 2000, año 84, a/c, motor, carrocería, llantas, excelente, recien traido. US$ 3.400. mejor oferta. tel. 2281570.

MAZDA B 2200, año 91, camioneta, rines de lujo, a/c, U$ 5000. telf. 2665716.

MAZDA B2200 '89 DE LUJO, GANGA. TEL:7772828

MITSUBISHI 4 Cilindro de gasolina año 89, extra cab. 260-3063

NISSAN '97, TINA, DIESEL. TEL: 278-5717, 088-67724.

NISSAN PATROL 4200, 1997, Diplomático vende; diesel, 66,000 kms; rojo, 7 pasajeros, full extras. Tel.: 268-0250-55

NISSAN STANZA 86, $2,000. 08860157

SUBARU S/W, 87, A/C, 4X4 U$3;300 NEGOCIABLE. TEL: 268-6775

TOTOYA año 72 Camioneta 12-R, U$ 2.000. Isuzu Pup año 81, U$ 3.000, negociable. telf. 077-64153,05227373.

TOYOTA 1980 probada $2400. Teléfono 2892025

LADA AÑO 94 con placas rojas de taxi. En buen estado. Tel: 270-1629.

LADA MODELO 1200 en buen estado. Tel.: 07788670.

MAZDA 323 año 97, a/c, doble alarma, radio pioneer, 44000kms. US$7,700. Extranjero vende. 2781640.

MAZDA AÑO 85, DEPORTIVO, COLOR NEGRO, SOLOS PARA GUSTOS EXCLUSIVOS. U$2,300 NEGOCIABLE. TEL.2442497

MERCEDES BENZ 190E año 92, automático, 4 cilindros, gasolina, full extras, excelente precio, excelente estado. Tel.: 08837027

MITSUBISHI LANCER 88 CON A/A, SEDÁN DE 4 PUERTAS EN BUENAS CONDICIONES. TEL.: 2801014, 2801768

MITSUBISHI TREDIA 88, automático. 2789759 / 08850853

MONTERO FULL EXTRAS AÑO 98 COLOR GRIS C/PLATA, DOBLE AIRE TEL: 248-0014/249-7103.

NISSAN 82, taxi, c/p, U$3,000.00. Tel:0311-2195. León. Me voy.

NISSAN MAXIMA 82, diesel, mecánico. 2789759 / 07777818

NISSAN SENTRA 86 $1900 negoc. 2481780 / 08861088

NISSAN SENTRA '94 Edición limitada extras. US$6,200. Tel.: 2661843.

NISSAN SENTRA año 87, A/C, U$2,800 negociables. Tel: 2222643/2601765

115

puting an arbitrary value on your vehicle. They have alist showing the manufacturer's suggested retail price of every vehicle made when it was new, including extra equipment.

Customs agents refer to the market value based on their "Black Book," a manual published in the U.S. with a listing of new and used car wholesale auction prices. The book is a bible for U.S. car dealers, loan officers and customs agents. For additonal information about the Black Book, contact National Auto Research at 2620 Barrett Road, PO Box 758, Gainsville, GA 30503. Tel: (770) 532-4111, Fax: (770) 532-4792, www.blackbookguides.com.

After reading the above, if you still decide to import a used vehicle, we recommend using a customs broker to run around, obtain all the necessary documents and massive paperwork and to help with the taxes. After going through this process a friend of ours told us, "A good customs agent can save you money. He can take you step-by-step through this whole ordeal."

Driving an Automobile to Nicaragua

If you have sufficient time and enjoy adventure, drive your automobile to Nicaragua. The journey from the U.S. to Nicaragua (depending on where you cross the Mexican border), takes about three weeks if driving at a moderate speed. (The shortest land distance from the U.S. to Nicaragua is about 2000 miles through Brownsville, Texas.)

Take your time so you can stop and see some of the sights. We recommend driving only during the day since most roads are poorly lighted if at all. At night, large animals—cows, donkeys and horses—can stray onto the road and cause serious accidents.

Your vehicle must be in good mechanical condition before

your trip. Carry spare tires and necessary parts. Take a can of gas and try to keep your gas tank as full as possible because service stations are few and far between.

Have your required visas, passports and other necessa ry papers in order to avoid problems at border crossings. Remember, passports are required for all U.S. citizens driving through Central America. You also need complete car insurance, a valid driver's license and a vehicle registration.

How to find a Lawyer

Nicaragua's legal system is based on civil law with the with the Supreme Court being able to review administrative acts.

If you paln to go into business, work, buy or sell property or seek long-term residency status in Nicargua, you will definitely need the services of a good attorney.

Your lawyer can help you understand the complexities of the Nicaraguan legal system. For instance, you are guilty until proven innocent, just the opposite of our system in the U.S.A. A good lawyer is one of the best investments you can make beacause he can assist you with bureaucratic procedures and handle other legal matters that arise.

If you are not fully bilingual, be sure to choose a layer who is. The secretary should be bilingual too(Spanish/English).This helps avoid communication problems and misunderstandings, and enables you to stay on top of your legal affairs.

It is very important to watch your lawyer closely since some lawyers in Latin America tend to drag their feet as bureaucrats do.

Never take anything for granted. Refuse to believe that things are getting done, even if you are assured they are. Check with your lawyer on a regular basis and ask to see your file to make sure he has taken care of business. As you might imagine, paper work moves slowly in Nicaragaua so you don't want a procrastinating lawyer to prolong the process.

When you first contact a lawyer, make sure he is accessible at all hours. Make sure you have your lawyer's office and home telephone numbers in case you need him in an emergency. If your lawyer is always in meetings or out of the office, this is a clear sign your work is being neglected and you have chosen the wrong lawyer.

You may need a specialist to deal with your specific case. Some people find it's a good idea to have several lawyers for precisely this reason.

Take your time and look around when you are trying to find an attorney. This should be fairly easy since we have included a list from which to choose. You should ask friends, foreign residents and other knowledgeable people for the names of their lawyers. Above all, make sure your attorney is recommended from a reliable source. Then try to inquirer about your potential lawyer's reputation, his work methods, and integrity.

If you find yourself in a jam before finding a lawyer, contact the American Embassy for assistance or see the list at the end of this section.

All over the world, there are always a few incompetent, unscupulous attorneys, so be careful with whom you are dealing before you make your final choice. Remember one of the most important people in your life in Nicaragua will be your lawyer, so it is imperative that you develop a good working relationship. It is inadvisable to select your lawyer soley on the basis of legal fees. Lawyer's fees, or *honorarios*, vary. Just because a lawyer is expensive doesn't mean he is good. Likewise, you shouldn't select an attorney only because his fees are low.

We recommend purchasing a copy of, *Diccionario de Términos*

Jurídicos by Enrique Alcazar. It is a complete English/Spanish dictionary of legal terms.

Here is a partial list of attorneys who have some North American clients:

Gloria Alvarado and Associates
Industrial property law, commercial law, banking law, international law/foreign investment, privatization, real estate, labor law, environmental law, commercial litigation
Address: Del lacmiel, 5c. arriba, 300 mts a la derecha, no. 75
Tel: 505-277-4028 and 278-7708; Fax: 505-278-7491
E-mail: alvasoc@ns.tmx.com.ni
Internet site: www.lexmundi.org/052.html

Emilio Barrios and Associates
Corporate law, international banking, business law, patents, trademarks, and civil litigation.
Address: Detrás Del Restaurante La Marsellaise, 1c. abajo
Tel: 505-278-0019; Fax: 505-278-6576
E-mail: barrios@ibw.com.ni

Guy José Bendaña-Guerrero and Associates
Intellectual property law, chemical patents, license negotiation, industry models, trade marks, patents, pharmaceutical patents, general intellectual property practice.
Address: Portón Antiguo Hospital El Retiro, 1c. al lago
Tel: 505-266-5696 and 266-5697; Fax: 505-266-8863
E-mail: guybengu@ibw.com.ni

Francisco José Boza Páiz and Associates
Business, fiscal and banking law
Parque Las Madres 1 C. al lago, Casa No. 1603
Tel: 505-266-8860 and 266-2374; Fax: 505-266-2374
Terencio García of Mayorga, Valdivia, Rivas, and Escobar

Corporate law, finance
Apartado Postal 2536, Managua
Tel: 505-268-2233; Fax: 505-268-2234

López Arguello, Morales & Associates
Patent and trade marks, foreign investment, banking, customs, foreign trade, real estate corporations, administrative, commercial, civil, labor and tax law, oil and mineral, agency and distribution agreements, insurance, litigation and arbitration
Address: Canal 2, 300 vrs al Oeste, 25 mts al Sur
Tel: 505-266-0803 and 268-3070; Fax: 505-268-0017

Alvaro Martínez Cuenca
General practice, trademarks and patents
Address: Centro Comercial San Francisco, H-5
Tel: 505-278-0330; Fax: 505-277-1032
E-mail: ccisa@sgc.com.ni internet site: sgc.com.ni/ccisa

Juan Alvaro Munguía A., Luis Chávez Escoto and Associates
Banking and security law, general corp., Commercial law, leasing & project finance, foreign investment, mergers & acquisitions, private & administrative law, telecommunications, mining/oil/gas, environmental, intellectual property and technology law, labor law, litigation and arbitration bankruptcy/product liability, pharmaceutical, general insurance, aviation & shipping law, taxation and customs law, real estate law.Address:
Address: Edificio Málaga, Plaza España (2nd Floor)
Tel: 505-266-4157 and 266-1211; Fax: 505-266-4156
E-mail: jmunguia@ibw.com.ni, internet site: www.lexmundi.org.

Courtesy of U.S. Embassy Managua Econ/Commercial Section Home Page: usembassy.state.gov/posts/nu1/wwwhcom.html

Foreign Embassies and Consulates in Nicaragua

The local branch of your embassy and or consulate can provide you with help in avariety of circumstances. They also have current information about the country's political and investment climate. In Nicaragua embassies and consulates are located in Managua.

Austria	Tel: (505) 266-3316
Belgium	Tel: (505) 222-3202
Canada	Tel: (505) 228-1304
Costa Rica	Tel: (505) 266-3986
Chile	Tel: (505) 266-0302
Denmark	Tel: (505) 268-0250
El Salvador	Tel: (505) 276-0160
Finland	Tel: (505) 266-7947
France	Tel: (505) 222-6210
Germany	Tel: (505) 266-3917
Great Britian	Tel: (505) 278-0014
Guatemala	Tel: (505) 279-9609
Honduras	Tel: (505) 279-8231
Italy	Tel: (505) 266-6486
Japan	Tel: (505) 266-8668
Mexico	Tel: (505) 278-4919
Netherlands	Tel: (505) 266-6175
Norway	Tel: (505) 266-4119
Spain	Tel: (505) 276-0966
Sweden	Tel: (505) 266-0085
Switzerland	Tel: (505) 277-3235
United States	Tel: (505) 266-6018

*For more listings consult the Nicaraguan phone book or call information at 112.

Nicaraguan Consulates and Embassies Abroad

The principla job of consulates is to issue visas, take care immigration matters and other official documents. They also have a wealth of information for anyone thinking of travelling to or living or investing in Nicaragua.

Belgium — Embajada de Nicaragua, 55 Av. de Wolvendael 1180, Brussels, Belguim Tel: 375-6434

Canada — Embajada de Nicaragua, 130 Albert St., Suite 407, Ottawa, Ontario, Ontario K1P 5G4 Tel: (613) 234-9361 and 234-9362, Fax: (613) 238-7666

Chile — Embajada de Nicaragua, El Bosque Norte0140, Depto. 33, Santiago, Chile Tel: 23-12-0-34, Fax: 22-92-5-69

Colombia — Embajada de Nicaragua, Carrara 4a No 75-73, Bogotá Tel: 271-7680, Fax: 217-0509

Costa Rica — Embajada de Nicaragua, Avenida Central No 2540, Barrio, California Across the street from Pizza Hut, San José, Costa Rica Tel: (506) 233-3479, Fax: (505) 221-5481.

El Salvador — Embajada de Nicaragua, 71 Avenida Norte y 1a Calle Poniente, No 164, San Salvador Tel: 246-662, Fax: 241-223

Germany — Embajada de Nicaragua, Konstantinstrasse 41 D-53179, Boon/2, Germany Tel: 362-505 Fax: 354-001.

Great Britian — Consulado de Nicaragua, 84 Gloucester Road, London SW 4PP, Great Britian Tel: 584-4365

RED TAPE

Guatemala — Embajada de Nicaragua, 10 Avenida 14-72, Zona 10, Guatemala City Tel: 374-262.

Honduras — Embajada de Nicaragua, Colonia Teypec, Bloque M-1, número 1130, Tegucigalpa, Honduras Tel: 324-290, Fax: 311-412

Mexico — Embajada de Nicaragua, Payo de Rivera 120, Lomas de Chapultepec, CP 11000,MexicoDF Tel: 520-4421

Netherlands — Embajada de Nicaragua, Zoutmanstraat 53-E, 2518 GM, The hague Holland Tel: 363-0967, Fax: 310-6869

Panama — Embajada de Nicaragua, Calle 50 y Avenida Federico Boyd, Panama City Tel: 696-721

United States (Washington DC) — Embajada de Nicaragua, 1627 New Hampshire Ave. N.W., Washington, DC, 20009 Tel: (202) 939-6570 or 939-6573, Fax: (202) 939-6542

United States (Florida) — Consulado de Nicaragua, 8370 West Flager St., # 220, Maimi, Florida 33144 tel: (305) 220-6900 or 220-6931, Fax: (305) 220-8794

United States (New York) — Oficina Consular de Nicaragua, 820 2nd Avenue, Suite 802, New York, new York 10017 Tel: (212) 983-1981 or 983-2446, Fax: (212) 983-2646

United States (New Orleans) — Consulado General de Nicaragua, World Trade Center N2, Canal Street, Suite 1937, New Orleans, Louisana 70130 Tel: (504) 523-1507, Fax: (504)523-2359

United States (Houston) — Consulado General de Nicaragua, 6300 Hilcroft, Suite 470, Houston, Texas 77081 Tel: (713) 272-9628, Fax: (713) 272-7131

United States (Los Angeles) — Consulado General de Nicaragua, 636 South Plymouth Boulevard, Los Angeles, California Tel: (213) 252-1170. Fax: (213) 252-1177

United States (San Francisco) — Oficina Consular de Nicaragua, 870 Market Street, Suite 1050, San Francisco, California 94102 Tel: (415) 765-6825, Fax: (415) 765-6826

5

STAYING BUSY AND HAPPY IN NICARAGUA

Some Sound Advice

Retirement or just living in another country for whatever reason often presents new challenges for people because perhaps for the first time they are confronted with having a plethora of leisure time and the problem of what to do to with it. As you will see throughout this chapter, Nicaragua is wonderful place to live. In addition to being relatively inexpensive there are many interesting activities to choose from.

In Nicaragua you have no excuse for being bored or inactive, unless you are just plain lazy. Even if you cannot pursue your favorite hobbies, you can get involved in something new and exciting. Best of all, by participating in some of the activities in this chapter, you will meet other people with common interests and cultivate new friendships in the process. You can even spend your time studying Spanish.

Many people you meet will also be expatriates, so you probably won't need that much Spanish to enjoy yourself. However, the happiest foreigners seem to be those who speak

Spanish. They are able to enjoy the culture more fully, mix with the locals and make new friends in the process.

Whatever you do, don't make the mistake of being idle. The worst thing you can do is spend all your time drinking. Over the years we have seen many fellow Americans fail to use their time constructively, and destroy their lives by becoming alcoholics while living in Central American countries—a few even died prematurely. So, use the information we have provided in this chapter, and take advantage of all the activities Nicaragua offers.

Books, Magazines and Newspapers

English Books, newspapers and some magazines are available in Nicaragua. As the number of foreigners increases more printed books,magazinesand newspapers in English will become available. Books may be ordered through Amazon.com or one of the other on-line bookstores and shipped to you by Nicabox, one of the country's private mail services. It's also a good idea to buyEnglish books in the States while visiting. We have a friend who buys about $500 worth of books each time he makes a trip to the States. You might want to start a book swapping club with other expats. Check the phone book for bookstores (*librerías*).

Libraries are scarce. In Managua there is the **Emily Dickinson Library** at the Nicaraguan North American Cultural Center (265-2743). The **Biblioteca Nacional Rubén Darío** (Tel: (505) 222-2722 E-mail: Binanic@tmx.com.ni) is located in the **Palacio Nacional de la Cultura**.

If you read Spanish there are three major Spanish language newspapers in Nicaragua. *La Prensa* is a pro govenrment publication which leans to the right. *El Nuevo Diario* is another publication. Finally, *La Barricada,* is the official organ for the

Why Did You Come Here? What Do You Do?

By Martha Bennett

There are several species of estranjeros living in Nicaragua for a variety of reasons and doing different things. They come to retire, for adventure, to invest or open a business, or to study with one thing in common: changing their life style.

There are tourists. Some come to appreciate the flora and the fauna, volcanoes and lakes, beaches and mountains, and observe the Nicaraguan culture. Others flock for sports: fishing, surfing, hiking and hanging out. Everything is available except snow sports. Cultural events may be added on to either group's activities. No one comes for the great food which has not inspired restaurants in other parts of the world. No matter, the ingredients are available to create your own cusine.

The people who park here for six months to life do these things and more. Missionaries come for Latin language and culture. Some men come looking for the women. This builds the men's egos and the girls like the upgraded standard of living.

Others of all ages come to test their luck by going into business. Some are college educated, who can't find, satisfactory jobs in North America. They are found in the tourist industry, working for international companies or teaching at an English language school. In many cases foreigners can start a buisness but can't take jobs from a Nicaraguan. There are regulations, but in Latin countries, these are worked around. A slower pace of life and close family ties appeal to people in high stress jobs who have children. They come for a change of atmosphere. The tightly knit community provides a healthier climate for raising children than in the states.

Retirees participate in many things. Some renovate a dream house. Some persue the World Wide Web. There are movies and many other activities to keep busy and happy. As the country becomes more popular and the foreign population grows it will be increasingly easier to find more things to do. The country club set graces swimming pools, and dines elegantly. One can study art, writing, language, pottery, gardening, and more. You can even do volunteer work.

Remember, living takes longer here. Time is spent finding things, fixing things, cutting red tape and avoiding long lines. But this pace allows more time for reading, observing, listening to music and just being. In Nicaragua, we are more human beings than human doings.

SandinistaParty.

An excellent multi-language newspaper, Central America Weekly, made its debut a couple of years ago. It is has sections in English, Spanish and German. The paper has good business tips and is distributed in all Cental American countries. To subscribe: Central America Weekly, SJO - 117, P.O. Box 0025216, Miami, FL 33102.Tel: (506) 296-5500 Fax:(506) 290-7923 sales@centralamericaweekly.com.

Television and Radio

Nicaragua's national Spanish TV channels are 2, 4, 6, and 8. As in the United States, Nicaragua has satellite cable television. A variety of American television channels provide viewing and entertainment at a low cost from **ESTESA**. You won't miss much TV while living in Nicaragua since this company offers local channels in Spanish as well as English channels including CBS, NBC, ABC, FOX, HBO, CNN, ESPN, TNT, the Discovery Channel and more. Cable modem service is available in some areas. ESTESA publishes a monthly guide with all of their programs for their subscribers. Their offices are in every major city and most towns in Nicaragua. To contact the main office in Managua call: Tel: (505) 277-0525, 278-0849, Fax: (505) 278-1127 E-mail: estesa@cablenet.con.ni or estesa@interlink.com.ni www.interlink.com/ni-estesa. In Granada call:552-7335. Their office is located in the center of the city.

DirectTV (GALAXY NICARAGUA), Hospital Monte España 70 meters to the lake, Managua Nicaragua (Tel: (505)270-6767,Fax:(505)278-7537,E-mail:ventas@directtv.com.ni) is available in Nicaragua. With this system you can receive up to 100 channels including "Pay Per View"(for watching special events). The cost has dropped considerably. The basic

A Mother's Day Gift for 110 Nicaraguans
or
Don't Steal a Pig in Nicaragua

A third of Nicaragua's female prisoners walked free recently in a bizzare amnesty enacted by Congress in honor of Mother's Day held on May 30th.

The amnesty covered about 110 of the 300 women in Nicaragua's prisons, including many convicted of murder, peddling drugs and theft.

During their last night at a women's prison outside Managua, a Mariachi band serenaded the jubilant prisoners from outside their cells. On Tuesday, the somber prison turned into a festive dance hall as the prisoners celebrated their new-found freedom with live music.

First lady María Fernanda de Aleman bid them farewell, passing out clothes and other household items to help them start their lives again.

"I'm going straight home to see my kids," said Sheila Marquez, a mother of four who served one year of a five-year sentence for allowing drugs to be sold out of her home. Others headed straight to the Metropolitan Cathedral to thank God.

"We are sure that they will never commit crime again," said congressman Nelson Artola, president of the congressional human rights commission.

Arola said most of the women were "victims of a society that gave them no options."

"We gave them their freedom because most were pushed toward crime by poverty and unemployment."

"Of the country's 6,000 prisoners, about 300 are women, the majority single mothers," Artola said.

The congress denied amnesty to the remaining women based on the seriousness of their crime and their behavior.

María Eugenia Espinoza, 33, has served seven years for murder, but was told she must complete her 12-year sentence. Cruz Angelina Gómez Hernández, a 36-year-old mother of five, will remain in prision awaiting trial on charges of stealing a pig.

installation cost is about $100 and $35 monthly for the basic package. Direct TV systems purchased in the U.S. will not work with the satellite systems in Nicaragua or the rest of Latin America. NFL and NBA sports packages are now available.

Most of Nicaragua's 30 or 40 radio stations play Latin music. **Radio 99.9** www.pirata.com., Managua plays good music. **Stereo Ya** (90.5FM) plays some North American pop music. As in the rest of Central America many of the bus drivers play the rock music that the English stations play.

Video Rentals

Video buffs will be happy that there are video rental shops doing business in Nicaragua's larger cities and towns. For a small initial fee you can acquire a membership at one of these stores and enjoy many privileges. Many movies you rent are in English with Spanish subtitles. **Video Centro** (249-5920), **Polanco's Video** (289-2060) and **Videocenter** ((278-8530) three places where you may rent videos in Managua. In Granada try **Video Laser** for your video rentals. It is located about two blocks from the main plaza.

Shopping

One way to keep active is to go shopping. Although Nicaragua is not as commercialized as the U.S., you can still spend your free time doing some serious shopping, browsing or just window shopping mainly in Managua.

For you mall-rats or mall-crawlers, there are also a number of new malls and shopping centers in the Managua area. Don't expect to find the type of mammoth mega-malls of the scale found in the U.S. or in neighboring Costa Rica. Check out **Metro Centro** on the south side of Managua's cathedral, **Centro Comercial Managua** and **Plaza Inter**. Metro Center is

STAYING BUSY AND HAPPY IN NICARAGUA

Nicaragua's mega-shopping mall and houses more than 80 business including McDonald's rival, Burger King. Plaza Inter has the Cinemas Inter movie theaters, La Plazcita food court and a variety of stores. **Plaza España** is another shopping center. U.S. style ministrip malls are also starting to appear.

La Curacao department stores are found all over the country. La Curacao has a total of 15 stores with 6 in the Managua area alone. They specialize in appliances and other articles for the home. If you don't want to bring your household goods from the States, you may buy almost everything you need in the Curacao.

General business hours run from about 8am to 5pm Monday through Friday. Larger shopping centers in Managua may have extended hours.

Because of the growing number of foreigners citizens living in Nicaraguans, and many Nicaraguans who have been exposed to U.S. culture by cable TV and visiting the States, there

Shopaholics will love the new Metro centro mega mall in Managua.

has been an influx of American products.

The only problem is that many of these goods are more expensive in Nicaragua because of import duties.

Everyday more and more imported goods from the U.S. are available in Nicaragua. Imported brand name cosmetics, stylish clothing, appliances and some foods, can now be found in many stores.

If you choose to live in Nicaragua, you may have to substitute many local products for items you ordinarily use and do without some other things. This is easy because of the variety of similar products available in Nicaragua.

If you absolutely must have products from the States, you can go to the U.S., Costa Rica or Panama every few months— as many foreigners and wealthy Nicaraguans do— to stock up on canned goods and other non-perishible foods, clothing, sundries and cosmetics. We know of one American retiree who goes to Miami every three or four months to buy all the goodies he can't find in Nicaragua. These frequent trips to the States may be unnecessary if you learn to make do with the local products.

One thing you may need some time to get accustomed to is the way purchases are handled in some stores. One clerk will wait on you, another will ring up the purchase and finally you will pick up your merchandise at another window. You find this system in most department stores, pharmacies and older businesses.

This system seems to create a lot of extra work for employees and delays for customers. The good news is that every day more and more stores are adopting the American style one-step self-service system.

Nicaragua does have excellent craftsmen so handycrafts and custom-made furniature are readily available in Nicargaua. The area around Masaya and local markets feature good places

STAYING BUSY AND HAPPY IN NICARAGUA

to shop. Many Cuban cigar makers set up shop in Estelí area where they produce export quality cigars in their factories. We know of several foreigners who have decorated their homes beautifully with pottery, paintings and word carvings.

Nicaraguan Pastimes

Nicargaua has a wealth of indoor and outdoor activities designed for everyone regardless of sex, age, personal taste or budget. Everyone—Nicaraguans, tourists and foreign residents—can participate in camping, walking, dancing, weight lifting, tennis, baseball, swimming and surfing, jogging, bicycling, horseback riding, and sailing. There are also art galleries, social clubs, museums and parks. Dedicated couch-potatoes can even stretch out and admire the lovely landscape or work on improving their suntans. There is something for everyone —so enjoy.

Gyms and health clubs are a good place to socialize and make new friends while working out. Some gyms even have spas, tennis courts and swimming pools. There are over 32 gyms in the metropolitan area. Call around and visit those in

Memebership is reasonable if you want to join a private country club.

your area to find out which is right for you.

Gimnasio Zeus is a gym near the center of the city of Granada which has weightlifting facilities. It costs about $10 monthly to belong to Granada's only gym. In Managua there are **Gimnasio Quick-Fit** Tel: (505) 265-2401 and **Gimnasio Atenas** (505) 283-1474. Please see the Managua phone book for more listings.

If you wish to join a private athletic club, country club or gym **Cocibolica Jockey Club** on the outskirts of Granada has a couple of swimming pools, a horse racing track and other facilities. The annual membership fee is around $2,000.

Museums and Art Galleries

In the Managua area there are a number of museums. The **Museo Nacional de Nicaragua** or National Museum (222-5291, 6886 E-mail: mnndc@ibw.com.ni) has historic and archeological exhibits and is open on weekdays. The **Museo Cortázar** (222-4449) offers painings, sculpture, engravings and

Expats can get in shape at Granada's Gimnasio Zeus.

drawings by Latin American artists.

Museo Casa Hacienda San Jacinto (222-6290 or 222-6200) displays objects from past centuries. Other museums are **Acahaulinca Footprints Museum** (Managua), **Museum de Alfabetzación** (Managua), **Museum of Anthropology and History** (Rivas) and **The Masaya Volcano Museum** (Masaya).

When in the city of León be sure to visit the Museo Rubén Darío (311-2388). This museum houses a library and a collection of the poet's manuscripts.

The themes reflected in Nicaraguan art include the country's natural environment, its geography, and its history, through which independence is depicted constantly. In Managua can visit the following galleries: **Códice** (277-1370), **Contil** (277-1370) and **Epikentro** (266-0959).

A Paradise for Watersports and Nature Lovers

Like Costa Rica and its other Cental American neighbors,

San Juan del Sur one of Nicaragu's beautiful beaches.

there are a wealth of outdoor activities for everyone in Nicaragua.

Nicaragua is sometimes called "the land of water." As we alluded to in Chapter 1, there a numerous beaches on the west coast which are perfect for swimming, surfing, boogieboarding, sailing and more. Snorkeling is best on the Caribbean coast especially around Corn islands.

Lake Nicaragua and especially the island of Ometepe has good beaches for swimming. There are also a couple of popular swimming spots a short distance from Managua. **Laguna de Xiloá** is a beautiful clear-water crater and is good for boating and swimming. **El Trapiche** is a swimming resort with large outdoor pools. Finally, there is **Laguna de Apoyo** which is another good place for swimming. All of these spots get crowded on weekends.

In the mountains North of Managua near Jinotega, is **Lago de Apanás**. It is popular for swimming and fishing. Sportsfishing is offered on the Pacific coast at San Juan Sur and Montlimar. There is good offshore fishing for swordfish all year round in some areas. **Cutting Loose Expeditions** (407 629-4700) in the U.S. offers fishing trips to Nicaragua. **Tico Travel** (**www.ticotravel.com** and **www.centralamerica.com**), the Central America experts, also have trips to the country.

Nicarauga is a nature lover's paradise. The country has its share of national parks and refuges to help protect its flora and fauna.

The **Selva Negra** forest in the mountains near Matagalpa and the islands in Lake Nicaragua are good for hiking. You can also hike or climb on the Masaya volcano and the two volcanos on Ometepe Island.

The Pacific side of western Nicaragua is flat, so it is perfect for touring on bicycle.

Baseball in Nicaragua

Baseball and not soccer is Nicaragua's most popular national game. The first official baseball game in Nicaragua was played in July of 1891. In 1935, Nicaragua took second place behind Cuba in the Central America and Caribbean games. The 1970s was considered to be the "golden age of Nicaraguan baseball." During this time the country produced six major league starswith Pitcher Denis Martínez as the most famous of the group. Managua named a national stadium to honor him when he retired.

There are stadiums in most large towns where you can sip on a local beer and take in a ball game. The season runs from October to April and pretty much coincides with the country's dry season.

We know one group of enterprising gringos who are thinking of sponsoring a major league team in Nicaragua. So far this is only a dream but has a good chance to become a reality in the not too distant future.

Baseball is Nicaragua's most popular sport.

Where to Make New Friends

You should have no problem making new friends of either sex in Nicaragua, but might have some difficulty meeting

Nicaraguans if you speak little or no Spanish. Some educated *nicas* speak English and dying for the chance to perfect their English language skills while you work on your Spanish. Perhaps you can find someone to exchange language lessons with. This is a good way to make new acquaintances and learn how Spanish is really spoken.

You most certainly will find it easier to meet fellow Americans in Nicaragua than in the U.S., because Americans living abroad tend to gravitate toward each other. Newcomers only have to find an enclave of fellow countrymen and they can make new friends. You can't help bumping into other Americans since Nicaragua is such a small country. This is especially true if you live in one of the areas like Granada, where many North Americans reside.

You have no reason to be lonely unless you want to be. Just be yourself and you will find Nicargaua is just the place for you.

As Nicaragua develops and the expat comunity grows, foreigners will be able to meet others who share the same interests. One way to keep busy is by linking people with common interests by forming a club. Here is a list of possible organizations you may want to start or join if some of them already exist:

American Legion Post
Poker Club
Backgammon Club
Book Club
Birdwatchers Club
Canadian Club
Canoe/Kayackong,

STAYING BUSY AND HAPPY IN NICARAGUA

> Sailing Club
> Chess Club
> Democrats Abroad
> Disabled American Veterans
> English-Spanish Conversation Club
> Fishing Club
> Hiking Club
> Internet Club
> Investment Club of Nicaragua
> Latin Dance Club
> Lions Club
> Mac User Group
> Mountain Bike Club
> Newcomers' Club
> Personal Computer Club
> Republicans Abroad
> Rotary Club
> Runners Club
> Spanish/English Conversation Club
> Square Dance Club
> Stamp Collectors Club
> T'ai Chi Chuan
> Video Club
> Women's Club of Nicaragua

Love and Permanent Companionship

If you are looking for someone for romance, Nicaragua might just be the right place for you.

Ladies, regardless of age, you will find gentleman admirers if you so desire. Due to *machismo*, Nicaraguan men are more flirtatious and aggressive than North American men. Most Nicaraguan men think foreign women have looser morals and are easier conquests than Nicargauan women. So, be careful to take time to develop a long-term, meaningful relationship and don't rush things.

Men of any age will have no problem meeting women. Central American women seem to like older, more experienced men. In some places it is not unusual to see a wife who is ten to twenty younger than her spouse. This practice may be frowned on in some countries but is usually accepted in Nicargaua. Many middle age foreigners and retirees we know claim to feel rejuvenated and to have a new lease on life after becoming involved with younger women.

In general, the ladies of Nicaragua are more warm-hearted and devoted than their North American counterparts. One retiree we know boasts, "The women here really know how to treat you like a king!"

A man doesn't even have to be rich to meet women—a $1,000 Social Security check translates to a millionaire's pay in Nicargaua. However, before becoming involved with a Nicaraguan woman, you should realize the many cultural differences that can lead to all sorts of problems, especially if you don't speak Spanish fluently.

Generally, Latin women are more jealous and possessive than American women, and tend not to understand our ways unless they have lived in the United States. Also, be aware that because of their comparative wealth, most Americans, especially the elderly, are considered prime targets for some unscrupulous Latin females.

In some cases there is another bad side of marrying a Latin woman in that you can end up supporting her whole family either directly or indirectly as many foreigners complain.

We advise you to give any relationship time and make sure a woman is sincerely interested in you and not just your money—you will save yourself a lot of grief and heartache in the long run.

Protitution is found in Managua as everywhere in the world. One can drive around in the dingiest areas or along clean avenues and see the women of the night displaying their wares. The police most often show indifference towards

STAYING BUSY AND HAPPY IN NICARAGUA

prositutes in Nicaragua. They know the ladies of the night have to earn a living. There is a common understanding that prostitutes are not doing this job to harm anyone or society but to survive.

Some prostitutes work the streets, others out of strip clubs and one group hangs out in good neighborhoods and around upscale hotels. Sex is available to men of all ages. Be careful of the ladies of ill-repute. Many foreigners after inviting one of these females to spend the night, have awaken the next day without the woman and minus wallets and other valuables.

Along the highways and on the outskirts of many cities and towns there are the famous love motels. These love nests can also be found in Costa Rica and other Central American countries. Basically, they provide a place where people can have everything from an afternoon fling to a long rendezvous. There is an hourly rate, so you may stay as long as you want.

Some men take prostitutes to these places while others take their secretaries lovers or a new friend.These places are very discreet. The carports usually have doors or curtains to hide a car's license plates and all contact with the employess of establishments is basically anonymous. You may sometimes order food and drinks at these places

Most single men can avoid getting involved with gold diggers, prostitutes, or other troublesome women if they know where to look for good women.

Many foreign men have knowingly and unknowingly married bad women. Some girls are honest and will directly ask you for money. The hustlers are more dangerous because their agenda is to really take you to the cleaners and they do not rule out marrying you to achieve this objective. Some men say that have lost everything from airline tickets that are cashed instead of used, large sums of money, girls claim they need to get visas, houses and more. These are the women who contribute to the bad stories you may hear about some Latin women. So falling in love with a bad girl will typically lead to a lot of heartache and problems. Unfortunately they are the easiest girls to meet in many instances and a good number of men fall into this trap.

A very small number of these women will become good wives, find religion, etc. They are often women who have been sexually or otherwise abused at a very young age so the problem is very deeply rooted. Your realistic chances of converting them are very slim, no matter how gorgeous the girl is, it is just not worth it.

The best way to spot a bad girl is her profile. They never have a job, never live with their parents, never have phone numbers and never invite you to their home or introduce you to their friends or family. They do not want to leave any trail for you to track them down later. They typically come from very poor backgrounds and have very little education, rarely completing high school. They are quite aggressive and target older Americans. Often they speak a little English and will start up a conversation with you or smile at you, until you make the first move. They will appear friendly and sincerely interested in you. They are always attractive or very young.

On the other hand a nice traditional Latino woman typically lives with her parents until she gets married. Single daughters are not encouraged to get jobs, unless the parents are very poor. Instead they are expected to help with taking care of the house or study.

All Nicaraguans value making new friends. Americans often misread this friendliness and think the woman has a romantic interest in them. In order for the women to develop any romantic interest in you at all, they have to first know from a trusted third party that you are looking for a long term relationship. After a brief encounter, a decent woman will

STAYING BUSY AND HAPPY IN NICARAGUA

never ask for your phone number. If you ask for her number, she will always give you the wrong number in order to avoid appearing rude. Nice women live with their parents and would never want to have strange guys calling their house. From a romantic interest point of view, quality Latin women are very difficult to meet.

If the woman is convinced you are seriously looking for a long term relationship she will then start to show an interest in getting to know you better.

In Costa Rica we know of one American we know ran an ad in the *Tico Times* and the local Spanish newspapers and ended up screening hundreds of women before finding his ideal mate. As far as we know he is still happily married. You might try this method in Nicaragua. Taking classes at a university is another way to meet quality women. If you have Nicaraguan friends, they will usually be able introduce you to someone worthwhile.

Furthermore, over the years we have encountered a lot of foreigners who end up not using common sense and end up getting involved with people with whom they would probably never associate back home. This brings us to the story of "Dumb and Dumber."

Dumb came to Central America about twelve years ago from the U.S. where he was a successful businessman. Almost upon arrviving here he became romantically involved with a woman of ill- repute. He was basically too lazy and busy getting drunk to to find a quality mate. Over the course of his relationship he lost about $300,000 because he entrusted his business dealings to his girlfriend. After splitting up with her and having to give her half of everything he owned because of their common law situation, he went and got involved with another much younger women who will probably "take him to the cleaners" someday.

Dumber is even stupider than dumb. He came to the country as a millionaire. The first thing he did was get romantically involved with a woman of the night. Dumber also spent most of his time in bars like Dumb. Consequently, when he broke up with his lady friend, after a few years together, he had to pay her around $50,000. He is now with another woman and most likely supporting her whole family. He'll probably end up broke like Dumb. Neither Dumb or Dumber speak Spanish nor have made an effort to understand the locals and constantly refer to them in derogatory terms.

The majority of foreign men who come to Central America don't share Dumb and Dumber's fate. Nevertheless they should learn a lesson from this story.

Note: The author of this guidebook feels it is his responsibility to paint a realistic picture of all of the aspects of living in Nicaragua.

TGIF Fridays is a place you can fun at in Managua.

He would not be doing a service to our readers if he didn't cover the subject of prostitution. However, let it be known that in no way does he condone the sexual exploitation of minors. In this section he only provides information about sexual relationships between consenting adults.

Nightlife and Entertainment

A night on the town in Managua can prove to be a lot of fun. In Managua the are many bars and night clubs which cater to people with money.

Try **La Buena Nota** (266-9797) for a laid-back atmosphere. Other good places to have a drink are: **Bar Arrecife** (278-0898), **Bar Las Conchas Negras** (228-0347), **El Chanán Bar** (278-6111) and **La Cavanga** (228-1098),

Nicaraguans, like most Latins love to dance. **Cats Club** (222-3232) is considered a top disco and has live music on weekends.

A local Expat hangout in Granada.

Stratos (2784013-) bills itself as the most modern discoteque in Managua. **Lobo Jack** (267-0124,) www.lobojack.com, is another happening spot. Also check out the **Mambo Cafe** (222-5539) near the Intercontinental Hotel. **Discotheque Cocojambo** (522-6241) at Complejo Turistico El Malecón, rocks all night long.

You may catch reggae music at **Mansión Reggae** (289-4804). The U.S. chain **TGIF Friday's** just opened a bar/restaurant in Managua.

SportsRock Cafe (267-0424) has 20 televisions and one with a giant screen. They serve a wide variety of American food, national and foreign alcoholic beverages, have a pool table, and great music.

In Granada check out **Hospedaje Central, Charley's International Bar, La Fábrica, Las Alemanas, Ceasrs** (located on the waterfront), **Café Subterraneo** or the bar at the **Hotel Alhambra** (552-4486).

In San Juan del Sur try **Marie's** bar/restaurant. **Harley Charlie's** is a new U.S. style sports bar with air conditioning and Direct TV.

Gamblers can enjoy themselves at one of the country's many casinos.

STAYING BUSY AND HAPPY IN NICARAGUA

If your're on atight budget there are still many bars where the locals drink and have a good time.

Gambling

Gambling is available in Nicaragua. Casinos are are found in several areas. **Josephine's** (222-6275 or 222-5134), in Managua bills itself as the best casino and night club in the country. **Fantasy Club** (249-7434 or 249-1714) and **Pharo Casino** are other casinos in the Managua area. There is also a small casino in Granada. The National Lottery is another form of gambling. It is very popular among the locals.

Movies and Theaters in Nicaragua

In most Nicaraguan cities you will find movie theaters. Managua has by far the best selection of theaters.Cinemark, which is an American movie chain which has U.S.-style-movie theaters in several Central American countries including Costa

Recently released movies with subtitles are shown in Nicaragua.

Rica, has invested in a theater in Nicaragua.

This state-of-the-art movie theater is found in the new MetroCentro shopping center. it has 6 screens and stadium-type seating. Other large theaters in the Managua area are **Cinema 1 & 2, Cinema Inter 1, 2, 3** and **4** at the **Plaza Inter** shopping center and **Cine América**.

In Granada the **Karawala** has two screens. **La Barba del Mono Hostal (The Bearded Monkey)** (505) 552-4028 shows movies every night. They also have internet facilities, a laundry and offer tourist information. You can meet a lot of interesting people by hanging out there.

You can however see a lot of movies on cable tv. You may want to start a collection of videos. We know several people in Nicaragua who do this and exchange them with friends.

6

COMMUNICATIONS

Telephone and Internet Services

Nicaragua's combined telecommunications provider and post office used to be called Telcor. In an effort to privatize the system, Telcor's name was changed to **Enitel**. Eventually, the govenrment plans to sell 40% of the company to foster growth. Another goal of the sale is to improve the nation's telephone system and meet the country's unsatisfied demand for telecommunications service.

Nicaragua currently only has three telephone lines per 100 inhabitants. The country needs to increase the number of telphone lines to 300,000 by the year 2002 — more than doubling the 140,000 lines now in use.

To obtain a telephone line go to any Enitil office. You can usually get a line in a few days. You'll need to make a deposit and have a person who already has a telephone to be reponsable for paying your bill in the event you don't pay.

There are public telephones in Managua, other major cities, and Enitel offices.

To call Nicaragua from abroad you'll have to first dial the country code before the local number. For example, from the U.S. you'll need to dial 011 + 505 + the local number.

International calls are possible from private phones, some hotels and any Enitel office. Most telephone offices are open from 8am to 10pm. If you call from an Enitel office, you must pay for the call on the spot.

When dialing an international call directly you'll need use the following coutry codes:

Canada   00 -44 + the area code + the local number
Germany   00 -49 + area code + the local number
Great Britian 00-44 + the area code + the local number
United States   001 + the area code + the local number

Check with an international operator for the country code of other nations. Call 110 to talk to an operator for local calls and 116 to talk to an international operator.

There are also ways to direct dial to the United States:

AT&T   164
AT&T   174 (direct dial calling card)
MCI   166
Sprint 161
Canada 168

Sending a Fax is very easy in Nicaragua. Just go to any Enitel office.

You may rent cellular phones. A $200 deposit is required. They accept Visa and MasterCard. Call (505) 278-4483, 278-4484 or 278-4485 or fax (505) 278-3811.

To get a cell phone line you'll have to contact a local representative of **Bell South** (505) 268-0345. They are Nicaragua's official cell phone company. There are plenty of lines and it only takes a day or two to get hooked up. You have to pay a deposit of around $60 for a line. Kodak, La Curacao and Supermercados La Unión are local representatives of Bell South.

COMMUNICATIONS

Useful Telephone Numbers

General Information Numbers	112
Domestic Long Distance	110
International Operator	116
Collect calls from public phones	112

Direct interantional calls 00 + country code + city or area code + the telephone number

Telegrams by phone	117

Fire: See the list for each town in the back of this guide.
Police: Same as above.
* Important numbers for each city are listed in Chapter 10.

Internet Cafes abound in Nicaragua.

Internet Services

Computer buffs will be pleased to know full Internet services are available in Nicaragua. As of September 2000 Nicaragua had almost 10,000 internet accounts.

In the last two years the use of the Internet has been one of the main goals for business growth and development in the region according to the experts.

IBW Internet Gateway is the largest internet provider in the country. They offer e-mail, web page design and network development, Tel: (505) 278-6328 or 278-6700 Fax: (505) 278-6370. See www.ibw.com.ni.

Nicanet offers technical support, web design and consultants services. Tel: (505) 278-5528, Fax: (505) 270-3361 e-mail:gerencial@nicanet.com.ni, www.nicanet.com. **Interlink** is another provider. Contact them at (505) 270-3030 or see www.interlink.com.ni. **Nodo Nicarao** also offers internet connections and other services Tel: (505) 228-3092, Fax: (505) 268-1565, e-mail; nicarao@nicarao.org.ni or www.nicarao.org.ni.

If you live in Granada like many other expats you'll want to contact **Computadoras de Granada** Tel/Fax: (505) 0552-3368 or elvisgra@ibw.com.ni. They are the local representative for IBW. Their office is located right off the main plaza in the heart of the city. They will send someone to your house to program your computer for internet service. They also run an internet café where you may rent computers by the hour. Incidentally, there are four or five other internet cafes in the downtown area of Granada.

Mail Service

Correos de Nicaragua, the country's postal system, offers postal services for both local and international correspondence. Their main office can be contacted at PBX: 222-2048 or see

COMMUNICATIONS

www.correos.com.ni.

Post offices may be found in all cities and most large towns. They offer regular mail service with home delivery, post office boxes, express mail, money tranfers, fax and other services. If you move to Granada you can call the local post office at 552-3331. It is located about a block from the center of town.

The yearly cost of a post office box is about $15.00 for a small box and $30.00 for a large box. To mail a 20-gram letter or a post card it costs about 25 cents to within Nicaragua; 45 cents to the other Central American countries; 55 cents to to the rest of the Americas; 80 cents to Europe and $1.00 to rest of the world.

However, you are better off using a private mail service to all of your international mail. **TRANS-EXPRESS/Nica Box** offers a variety of services including physical address in Miami. What this means is that everything may be mailed directly to your Miami address and brought directly to you without ever passing through the Nicaraguan postal system.

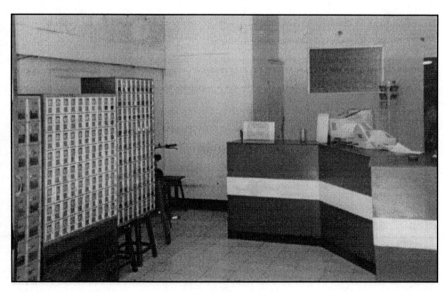

Local post offices offer many basic services.

You can avoid untimely delays, lost correspondence and other inconveniences. They also have a customs service for items on which duty must be paid. The customer doesn't have to to deal directly with Nicaraguan Customs which will save you time and headaches.

They offer home-delivery in Managua and plan to open branch offices in Granada and several other cities soon. They will also have an on-line way to track and monitor your account and corespondence.

Presently they have about 350 clients in the Managua area.

By using this handy service you won't have to worry about not receiving your favorite U.S. magazine or best-selling books from amazon.com.

You basically pay a monthy fee and are charged by the weight of anything you send or receive from abroad. For additional information contact: **NicaBox** Tel/PBX: 505-222-2270/222-6352, Fax:505 222-7588, E-mail: martham@nicabox.com.ni or see www.nicabox.com.ni or www.transexpress.com.

Receiving Money from Abroad

Do you plan on having money from abroad sent to you in Nicaragua? The fastest and safest way to receive money while visiting or residing in Nicaragua is to have an international money order or any other type of important document shipped to you by one of the worldwide courier services, such as **DHL** (228-4081), **UPS** (266-4289), **Federal Express** (266-2988) and **Western Union** (505) 266-8126. Letters and small packages usually take about two working days (Mon.–Fri.) to reach Costa Rica from the United States or Canada.

Other air couriers have offices in Managua: **Gigante Express** (278-2959), **Real Express** (263-1413), **Jetex** (268-2584) and **Jet**

COMMUNICATIONS

Box (268-0597). The Nicaraguan phone book has a list of more companies which offer similar services.

Western Union in Nicaragua boasts that they offer the fastest money transfers in the country. They have about 20 offices located around the country.

In Managua you may also contact Western Union at www.teledata.com.ni/westernunion for additional information. You'll have to show some form of valid identification to pick up your money.

U. S. banks can wire money to banks in Nicaragua. You can always have a trustworthy friend or relative bring you up to $10,000 when they come to Nicaragua.

Automatic Teller Machines (ATMS) are found all over the country. You can't transfer money directly but can get cash advances from one of your credit cards. This is along with cashing a personal check is perhaps the fastest way to get money. Credomatic now has ATM machines in Granada for your convenience..

Foreigners can count on Nicabox for all of the postal related needs.

Another safe way of having checks sent to you is through **Nica Box,** the private mail services we list in this chapter.

As in most foreign countries, you can have Social Security and Veteran's benefits mailed to you directly through the U.S. Embassy, once you have established a permanent residence in Nicaragua

However, these checks usually don't arrive until sometime after the tenth of each month.

Correos de Nicaragua, is another option. They offer **EMS** a courier service and **$TD** money tranfer service. They claim that the services are reliable and safe. However, you're probably better off using a private company.

EDUCATION

How to Learn Spanish

Although many well-educated Nicaraguans speak English, Spanish is the official language. Anyone who seriously plans to live or retire in Nicaragua should know Spanish — the more the better. Frankly, you will be disadvantaged, handicapped and be considered a foreigner to some degree without Spanish. Part of the fun of living in another country is communicating with the local people, making new friends and enjoying the culture. Speaking Spanish will enable you to achieve these ends, have a more rewarding life and open the door for many new, interesting experiences. Knowing some Spanish also saves you money when you're shopping and, in some cases, keeps people from taking advantage of you.

If you take our advice and choose to study Spanish, for a modest fee you can enroll at one of Nicaragua's intensive conversational language schools. In addition to language instruction, most of these schools offer exciting field trips, interesting activities and room and board with local families— all of which are optional. Living with a family that speaks little—or preferably no—English is a wonderful way to improve your language skills, make new friends and learn about

Nicaraua's culture at the same time.

Spanish is not a difficult language to learn. With a little self-discipline and motivation, anyone can acquire a basic Spanish survival vocabulary of between 200 and 3000 words in a relatively short time. Many Spanish words are similar enough to English, so you can guess their meanings by just looking at them. The Spanish alphabet is almost like the English one, with a few minor exceptions. Pronunciation is easier than in English because you say words as they look like they should be said. Spanish grammar is somewhat complicated, but can be made easier if you are familiar with English grammar and find a good Spanish teacher. Practicing with native speakers improves your Spanish because you can hear how Spanish is spoken in everyday conversation. You will learn many new words and expressions not ordinarily found in your standard dictionary.

Watching Spanish television and listening to the radio and language cassettes can also improve your Spanish. We suggest that if you have little or no knowledge of spoken Spanish, you purchase the one-of-a-kind Spanish Survival book and accompanying cassette advertised in this book. It is designed especially for people planning to retire, live or do business in Central America. It makes learning easy because the student learns the natural way, by listening and repeating as a child does—without the complications of grammar. If you are interested in a deeper study of Spanish, we are including a list of language schools at the end of this section. Please check first with the school of your choice for current prices.

The Spanish spoken in Nicaragua is basically standard Castillian Spanish except for one big difference which confuses beginning students. Spanish has two forms for addressing a person—*usted* and *tú*. However, in Nicaragua *vos* is used instead of *tú*. The verb form used with vos is formed by changing the r at the end of a verb infinitive to s and adding

Super Tips for Learning Spanish

by Christopher Howard M.A.

1) Build your vocabulary. Try to learn a minimum of five new words daily.
2) Watch Spanish TV programs. Keep a note pad by your side and jot down new words and expressions. Later use the dictionary to look up any words and expressions you don't understand.
(3) Pay attention to the way the locals speak the language.
(4) Listen to Spanish music.
(5) Talk with as many different Spanish speakers as you can. You will learn something from everyone. Carry a small notebook and write down new words when you hear them.
(6) Read aloud in Spanish for five minutes a day to improve your accent.
(7) Try to imitate native speakers when you talk.
(8) Don't be afraid of making mistakes.
(9) Practice using your new vocabulary words in complete sentences.
10) When you learn something new, form a mental picture to go along with it—visualize the action.
11) Try to talk in simple sentences. Remember, your Spanish is not at the same level as your English, so simplify what you are trying to say.
12) If you get stuck or tongue-tied, try using nouns instead of complete sentences.
13) Remember Spanish and English are more similar than different. There are many cognates (words that are the same or almost the same in both languages).
14) Learn all of the basic verb tenses and memorize the important regular and irregular verbs in each tense.
15) Study Spanish grammar, but don't get bogged down in it.
16) Read the newspaper. The comic strips are great because they have a lot of dialog.
17) It takes time to learn another language. Don't be impatient. Most English speakers are in a hurry to learn foreign languages and get frustrated easily because the process is slow. Study a little bit everyday, be dedicated, persist and most of all enjoy the learning process.
¡Buena suerte! Good luck!

Getting a Head Start

by Christopher Howard M.A.

If you are seriously considering moving to a Latin American country, you should begin to study Spanish as soon as possible.

Here are a few suggestions that will give you a head start in learning the language. Look for some type of Spanish course that emphasizes conversation as well as grammar and enroll as soon as possible. University extensions, junior colleges and night schools usually offer a wide range of Spanish classes.

You should also consider studying at a private language school like Berlitz if there is one near where you reside. Many of these schools allow the students to work at their own pace.

Another excellent way to learn Spanish, if you can afford it, is to hire a private language tutor. Like private schools this type of instruction can be expensive, but is very worthwhile. The student has the opportunity of working one-on-one with a teacher and usually progresses much faster than in a large group situation.

If you happen to reside in an area where there are no schools that offer Spanish classes, you should go to your local bookstore and purchase some type of language cassette. This way, at least you will have a chance to learn correct pronunciation and train your ear by listening to how the language is spoken.

Listening to radio programs in Spanish and watching Spanish television are other ways to learn the language, if you are fortunate enough to live in an area where there are some of these stations.

You can also spend your summer or work vacations studying Spanish in Mexico or Costa Rica. This way you will experience language in real life situations. These language vacations can be enjoyable and rewarding experiences.

Finally, try befriending as many native Spainsh speakers as you can who live in the area where you reside. Besides making new friends, you will have someone to practice with and ask questions about the language.

By following the advice above and making an effort to learn the language, you should be able to acquire enough basic language skills to prepare you for living in a Spanish speaking country. Best of all, you will acquire the life-long hobby of learning a new language in the process.

EDUCATION

2001
Costa Rica Books Catalog
More Great Books To Buy!

These highly specialized guides are available through our catalog.
On special request some can be ordered from bookstores
in the U.S. Canada or Europe.

"Living and Investing in the 'NEW' Cuba"
by Christopher Howard

ONE-OF-A-KIND *"The First and Only Guide to Living, Making Money and the Good Life in CUBA of the Future."*

This easy-to-use 270 page guidebook will bring you up to date on what is happening now and what the future will hold for Cuba. It is jam-packed with 'secret' insider information plus all of the ins and outs and dos and don'ts of living and investing in Cuba.

Order a copy today!

Speak Spanish Like a Costa Rican
by the author of
THE GOLDEN DOOR TO RETIREMENT AND LIVING IN COSTA RICA, Christopher Howard.

"A must if you plan to live in Costa Rica." Best-selling book, 90 minute cassette included!

**FAST, EASY, PROVEN METHOD!
GUARANTEED RESULTS!**

Living and Investing in the "New Nicaragua"
by Christopher Howard

"This visionary work will help anyone thinking of living or making money in Nicaragua. It promises to become a Cassic."

This ione-of-a-kind guidebook provides you with all the tools for living and investing in Nicaragua - Central America's "Sleeping Giant" and land of opportunity

161

The Legal Guide to Costa Rica
by Rodger Peterson, Attorney at Law

"This is a comprehensive guide to understanding and maneuvering within the Costa Rican legal system. It answers most of the questions you may have."

This practical books contains basic information on the most common legal situations which you will encounter in Costa Rica. It covers Real Estate transactions Forming Corporations. Commercial transactions, Immigration, Labor Laws, Taxation, Wills, Trademarks, Marriage and much more.

Driving the Panamerican Highway to Mexico and Central America
by Raymond Pritchard

CAR - RECREATIONAL VEHICLE - CAR & TRAILOR

This book tells you:

Safest routes to take; En route sightseeing; Border Searches - What to expect; Servicing you car en route; How to figure your costs in advance; Hotels, motels - Where to stay; Plus details of actual trip.

■ ■ ■ ■ ■ ■ ■ ■ ■ ■ ■ ■ ■ ■ ■ ■ ■ ■ ■

ORDER TODAY

* These books are not available in bookstores in the U.S. or Canada

☐	Living and Investing in the "NEW" Cuba	$ 24.95
☐	Living and Investing in the "New Nicaragua"	$ 24.95
☐	The Legal Guide to Costa Rica	$ 29.95
☐	Costa Rican Spanish Survival Course (Book & 90 minute Cassette included)	$ 14.95
☐	Driving the Panamerican Highway to Costa Rica	$ 9.95

Send to: Costa Rica Books   Add $3.00 Postage & Handling to U.S.
Suite 1 SJO 981, P.O. Box 025216   Canada & Latin America. $5.00 to Europe
Miami, FL 33102+5216   *All monies must be in U.S. dollars

ADD $ 1.00 FOR EACH ADDITIONAL BOOK • 619-461-6131
For addition information see:
www.costaricabooks.com • www.liveincostarica.com

an accent to the last syllable. This form is seldom taught because it is considered a colloquial form; used only in Central America and some parts of South America (Argentina and Uruguay). It is not found in most Spanish textbooks.

Another trait of the Nicaraguans is the common use of *don* (for a man) and *doña* (for a woman) when addressing a middle age or older person formally. These forms are used with the first name — as in the case of the famous "don Juan." However, you will usually hear the more traditional *señor* or *señora* used instead of *don* or *doña*.

Don't worry! Once you live in Nicaragua for a while and get used to the Nicaraguan way of speaking, you will learn to use the *vos* form almost automatically. If you do makes mistakes and use the *tú* form, most Nicaraguans overlook it because they know you are not a native speaker. Nicaraguans appreciate any effort you make to speak their language.

You will notice that Nicaraguans frequently use local expressions that are not used in other Latin American countries. We have listed a few in this chapter.

For some basic Spanish phrases see the section in Chapter 10 titled "Important Phrases and Vocabulary."

Spanish Language Schools

Nicaraguan Spanish Schools(N.S.S.) has an excellent total immersion Spanish language program program at all of its camupuses. Each location has its own beauty and unique physical and cultural envirnoment. The school presently has campuses in León, Granada and San Juan del Sur.

They offer courses of any duration and for all levels. Their programs are for indididuals, couples, families and groups. Class size is small and students study 4 hours daily Monday through Friday from 8:00am to 12:00 noon. Individualized tutoring is available for those students who want additional

Frequently Used Nicaraguan Expressions

Carambada — A thing
En pirinola — Broke, no money
Guaro — Moonshine
Estar chicle — Finished, washed up
Calentar banca — Seated
Chunche — Also a thing
Carajada — Another word for thing
Chillante — Shiny
Biscoreto — Crosseyed
Chuzo — Smooth
Pachón — Hairy
Chinear — Spoil a kid
Amorriñarse — To get sick
Echar pie atrás — Return
Tantear — To try something, experiment
Largo - Far (distance)
Ligero — Fast
Por el culo del mundo — Far away
A todo mamón — At full speed
A calzón quitado — Frankly, honestly
Caer como patada de mula — To cause a bad impression
Quedarse como la novia de tola — To get stood up by someone
A pata — On foot
En piña — In a group, collectively
Darle vuelta — To be unfaithful to someone
Tener leche — To be lucky
Parar la oreja — To listen
Quedarse zorrito — To keep quiet

EDUCATION

more intensive instruction.

Private homestay with a Nicaraguan family is included in the basic program and highly recommended as a part of the immersion process for accelerated language acquisition. This is a great way to know the people and customs of the country.

They also offer exciting weekend trips and excursions at each school for a low additional cost. As you already know, Nicaragua is the land of lakes and volcanoes and there are a variety of interesting places to visit near each school location.

This program has transferable university credits for strudents, teachers and professionals.

The cost for the basic program is: 1 week $195, 2 weeks $365, 3 weeks $535, 4 weeks or more $175 each; Tutoring $7 per hour. Subtract $60 per week for no homestay.

For additonal information contact: **Nicaraguan Spanish School**, Apartado SL-145, Managua, Nicaragua. Tel: In the U.S. 805-687-9941, in Nicaragua (505) 244-4212 (from USA first dial 011), E-mail: nss-pmc@prodigy.net or nssmga@ibw.com.ni, http://pages.prodigy.net/nss-pmc/. The Granada campus may be contacted at: E-mail: nss-pmc@prodigy,net. See their Website at http://pages.prodigy,net/nss-pmc/granada. Information from the ther campus may be obtained from their web pages.

Centro Cultural Nicararguense Norteamericano offers Spanish for Foreigners. Tel: (505) 265--2741, 265-3058, Fax: (505) 265-2727, E-mail: ccnn@uni.edu.ni.

Instituto de Español "Huellas" offers Spanish for foreigners. Choose time, course and place. Tel/Fax: (505) 266-7541, 266-7407 E-mail: espano@ibw.com.ni.

Centro Lingüístico Cultural "Tenotzani" Tel: (505) 687-9941 also has Spanish courses.

Escuela Horizonte in Estelí Tel: (505) 713-4117.

INCAE in Managua Tel: (505) 2 584 46/8.

Additional information about the above schools may be found by contacting **WorldWide Classroom**, Box 1166 - Milwaukee, WI 53201-1166, Fax: (414) 224-3466.

Nicaragua's Institutions of Higher Learning

Nicaragua's two main universities are the **Central America University** (Universidad de Centroamérica - UCA) in Managua Tel: (505) 2 78-3929 and the **National Autonomous University of Nicaragua** (Universidad Nacional Autónima de Nicaragua - UNAN) also in Managua Tel: (505) 270460.

Universidad Americana is another good university. Foreigners who are applying must meet the same requirements as regular students and provide the same documents which must be authenticated by a Nicaraguan Consulate in their country. For more information contact: Universidad Americana Tel: (505) 278-3800 E-mail: correo@uam.edu.ni, www.uam.edu.ni.

In Granada there is the **Universidad de Occidente** or UDO (505) 552-6325.

If you wish who wish to continue your education, you will have to find out what the requirements are for foreign students, if they offer courses in English and if course work is recognized in your home country.

MORE UNIVERSITIES

- National University of Agriculture Managua Tel:(505)21-16193
- National Universiyt of Engineering Managua Tel: (505) 2 7 1650

EDUCATION

Private Elementary and High Schools

If you have small children or teenagers you will be pleased that Nicaragua has a variety of schools to choose from. There are many public schools and a couple of bilingual American-style schools.

Public schools tend to be crowded, run down and leave a lot to be desired. Legal foreign residents are entitled to attend public schools. However, since all instruction is in Spanish, you shouldn't even think of enrolling your children in a public school unless they speak, read and write Spanish fluently. If your children are not Spanish speakers you have to enroll them in a private English school.

The American Nicaraguan School has an acredited academic program.

Nicaragua's private English-language schools are good and have high academic standards and are accredited in the U.S.

These schools are academically oriented and prepare students for admittance to colleges in the U.S. as well as in Nicaragua.

They teach English as a primary language and offer Spanish as a second language. In some ways these schools are better than similar institutions in the U.S.A., because not as many harmful distractions or bad influences exist in Nicaragua. Children also have the opportunity to learn a new language which is great value to them. The cost of some of these private schools can be more than $250 per month.

It is a good idea to visit a number of schools before deciding which one is right for your child. You should ask to visit a couple of classrooms as well as see all of the physical plant. This way you may view the schools infrastructure. Make a list of the pros and cons of each school before making your final decision. Don't forget to see if the school is accredited in the U.S. Also find out about the teacher /student ratio.

Be sure to see what percentage of the students graduate and go on to universities in Nicaragua, other Central American countries and the U.S. Finally, try to talk to other foreigners who have children enrolled in private schools to see if they are satisfied with the quality of education their children are receiving.

We talked with one couple from the U.S. who didn't have the resources to afford a private school so they opted for home schooling. They recommended several programs which you can find on the Internet: **www.calvertschool.edu**, **www.unl.edu** and **www.keystonehighschool.com**.

There are special courses of Spanish as a second language for students new to the country and advanced classes for

EDUCATION

foreign students and Costa Ricans who have mastered the language. We have seen children who move to the country learn to speak fluent Spanish in a couple of years. Conversely, Nicaraguan children are able to master English in a short period of time. If you listen to the high school students speak English you would think they grew up in the U.S. or Canada. It must be pointed out that, generally, the younger the student, the more quickly a second language can be learned. Junior and senior high school students take much longer to learn a new language than preschool and elementary students.

The following schools are accredited in the U.S. Some follow the U.S. schedule, September to June. Others follow the Nicaraguan academic year which begins in March and ends in November:

The American Nicaraguan School is the best bilingual school in Nicaragua. It is a private, coeducational institutuion and was founded in 1944. The school provides the best aspects of an American education and accredited curriculum to students pre-Kinder through grade 12. The school has 1,400 students from 27 nations. Thirty seven percent are from the U.S., forty-one percent are from Nicarauga and twenty-two percent are from tother nations. The school sits on a 26 acre campus in Managua, Nicaragua, and has 80 well-equipped, air conditioned classrooms, a library media center, computer and science laboratories, extensive athletic facilities for track and field, soccer, tennis, basketball, swimming, baseball and volleyball. A new Technology Center has CD-ROM and Internet access.The school follows a modified U.S. academic calendar.

When the author of this book toured the school he was very impressed with everything he saw.

The school community includes members of the diplomatic corps, members of foreign and local businesses. members of the Nicaraguan government and members of various foreign assistance groups working in Nicaragaua.

For additional information: **American Nicaraguan School**, Nicabox 192, P.O. Box 527444, Miami, FL 33152-7444 or P.O. Box 2670, Managua, Nicaragua, Central America Tel/Fax: (505) 278-2565 E-mail: mnormandin@cablenet.com.ni. Mary Ellen Normandin is the director of the school and will be happy to help you.

If you choose to live in Granada the American Nicaraguan School provides bus service from Granada to Managua for all students.

Lincoln International Academy is a Catholic, private, co-ed school with instruction in English. Lincoln follows the American educational system and offers Pre-school, elementary and High School levels, as well as SSL (Spanish as a secon language) and ESL (English as a second language). For more information: Lincoln International Academy, Nicabox #250, P.O. Box 52-7444, Miami, FL 33152 or Apt. Postal: UAM #296, Managua Nicaragua, Tel: PBX (505) 265-1521, Fax: (505) 265-3184 E-Mail; lincoln@interlink.com.ni www.lincoln.edu.ni.

The **Notre Dame School** Tel: 505 276-0354, Fax: 505 276-0416 is another bilingual school worth checking out.

Colegio Nicaragüense Frances Tel: 505 265-0526, 265-2410 Fax: 505 265-2426 has preschool, elementary and high school classes in French. They offer a complete academic program and even teach English at the high school level.

Colegio Alemán Nicaragüense Tel: 505 265-8449 Fax: 505 265-8117Carretera Sur Km 10 1/2 800 metros al Sur, offers a complete academic program with classes in German and Spanish.

See the Nicaraguan phone book for more listings of private schools.

GETTING AROUND

Air Travel to, in, and around Nicaragua

Augusto Sandino Airport, 8 miles outside of Manauga, is the country's main airport. It is small by international standards but offers all of the basic services. A number of major international airlines have flights to and from Nicaragua.

Most airlines offer excursion rates and three-or-four week packages. Fares are subject to availability, change and restrictions including advanced purchase requirements, minimum stops or cancellation penalties. Remember, the main tourist season in Nicaragua runs from about Thanksgiving to Easter. This period approximately coincides with local vacations so sometimes it is hard to find available space at this time of year. If you are planning to travel to or from Nicaragua during December you may have to buy a ticket months in advance because of the Christmas holidays. However, if you get into a jam you can sometimes find space on a flight via Costa Rica or Panama.

If you plan to travel or explore South America from Nicaragua you can usually save money by flying to Miami first and then buying a round-trip ticket to your destination.

Tico Travel (800-493-8426) specializes in trips to Nicaragua. We highly recommend this agency for booking your trip to Nicaragua or anywhere in Central America.

International Airlines Located In Nicaragua

Aeroflot	266-3588
TACA	266-3136
COPA	267-5438
AVIATECA	266-3136
LACSA	266-3136
NICA	266-3136
Air France	266-2612
Alitalia	266-2612
American	266-3900
British Airways	266-8268
Continental	263-1030
Nica	266-3136
Iberia	266-4440
KLM	266-8522
Lan Chile	266-7011
LTIU	266-7332
United	266-6663
Varig	266-2612

Domestic Airlines

There are small airports for domestic flights to Bluefields, Corn Island and Puerto Cabezas. Smaller domestic airlines, called charters are used for flights within the country.

Aeronautica Civil 244-4799

Traveling by Bus in Nicaragua

The city of Managua has afordable bus service. When

A Travel Business is Born
By Robert Hodel

So there I was, preparing for the culmination of three years of law when I realized that sinking feeling just was not going to go away.

That feeling I was referring to was the fact that I did not want to spend the rest of my life, nor even one minute for that matter, as a lawyer.

As soon as I accepted that fact I was in a quandry. What was I to do?

It was then I remembered from somewhere that the key to any successful business venture one may choose is to: 1) do what you like and 2) do what you know or do well.

With that in mind I pondered my future both day and night. Finally, I realized the thing I liked most to do was travel and the place I knew best, other than my home town, was Costa Rica.

I knew where was the best place to go and when. I also knew how to get the best prices on airfare, rental cars and hotels. So after a long phone call with my brother, who was even more knowledgeable than myself, I had a plan.

We would start a travel company dedicated primarily to Costa Rica and we would call it Tico Travel. I would move back to Costa Rica and introduce myself to the hotels, car rental companies and tour operators that we wanted to work with plus stay on top of any new developments that would be of interest to our clients. My brother moved to Florida and opened our office.

Within a short amount of time we became the agency of choice for people that travel frequently to Costa Rica and also for the first time visitor.

We also found no matter how much we advertised, that over 80% of our clients were either clients' referals or repeat customers, as a testimony to how important one's reputation is in this part of the world.

I have been told many times that one could make many times more money with the same effort if we were in the United States.

That may be so but I have been told something else by a longtime resident here,"We are not here for the money, we are here for the lifestyle."

Now we are branching out to Nicaragua. We have just purchased a couple of homes in Granada which we have begun to renovate and will turn into small hotels in anticipation of Nicaragua's boom in tourism.

See Tico Travel on the Internet at www.ticotravel.com. They now offer tours to Nicaragua.

you learn your way around you will find it easy to get to where you are going.

From Managua there are buses to most cities and towns in Nicaragua. Schedules can vary, so it is best to check before you travel.

Bus Travel to and from Nicaragua

You can travel to and from other Central American countries. Several companies offer these services. Nica Bus (Tel:505 228-1373. 228-1383) travels to and from Nicaragua. In Managua Nica Bus is located three blocks from the Cabrera movie theater. Transnica (278-2090)offers luxurious air conditioned buses with service from Managua to San José, Costa Rica. Tica Bus (222-3031 or 222-6094) has to several Central American countries.

Nicaragua's Taxis

Taxis operate in most major cities and towns of Nicaragua and are the easiest and safest way to travel. The country's buses are cheaper but taxis are the best way to get from point A to point B.

Taxis have no meter (*taxímetro*), so you'll have to negociate the cost of the trip before you get in. Sometimes you can bargain with the driver, but rates are often fixed. If you want the driver to wait while you do an errand or some other business, there is an hourly rate. If you have to go outside of a metropolitan area, there is another rate. In this case the driver and the passenger should negotiate the fare (Do this in advance). Be aware that rates are higher after dark.

Taxis can be found around every public square and park, outside restaurants, on most busy streets and in front of

GETTING AROUND

government buildings and most hotels. It is difficult to find a cab during the rainy season, especially in the afternoon when it usually rains. You may also have trouble getting a cab weekdays during rush hour between 7 a.m. and 9 a.m. and 4:30 p.m. to 6:30 p.m.—as in most cities. To hail a cab just yell, "Taxi!" If a cab is parked just say "ocupado" (free) to the driver to see if a cab is available. If the cab is available, he will usually nod or say, "sí" (yes).If you want to stay on a cab driver's good side, NEVER slam the taxi's doors; cabs are expensive in Nicaragua or any other Central American country and drivers try to keep them in good shape.

If you call a cab, be able to give your exact location in Spanish so the taxi driver knows where to pick you up. If your command of Spanish is limited, have a Spanish speaker write down directions to your destination. We know one old grouchy gringo who has never made an effort to learn a word of Spanish. He uses this mehtod of having all the directions of the places he has to go written in Spanish for cab drivers.

Taxis are plentiful and inexpensive in Nicaragua.

Airport pick-ups can be arranged in advance by calling one of the cab companies. We recommend doing this, especially during the rainy season, when it is difficult to get a cab when you need one.

> Here is a list of several taxi companies in Managua
> Cooperativa Carlos Fonseca Amador 222-7937
> Cooperativa de Taxi 25 de Febrero, R.L.......... 222-5218
> Cooperativa 2 de Agosto.................263-1512, 263-1839

Automobile Rentals

While exploring Nicaragua you may choose to rent an autombile. Major international car rental agencies and private car rentals are are found in Nicaragua. Most rental agencies operate like those in the United States. The cost of renting a vehicle depends on the year, model and make of car. You must be at least 18 years old and have a valid driver's license, an American Express, Visa or Master Card or be able to leave a large deposit. Remember, insurance is extra. Always phone or make arrangements for car rentals well in advance.

> Auto Express 222-3816
> Avis 233-3861
> Budget 263-1222
> Dorado...233-1329
> Hertz 233-1237
> Hundai 278-1249
> Leo's 266-9719
> Targa..233-1176
> Toyota 233-2192

GETTING AROUND

Driving in Nicaragua

You can drive from the States or Canada to Nicaragua. If you decide to make the journey purchase th e guidebook, *Driving the Pan-American Highway to Mexico and Central America*. You can now order this one-of-a-kind book by writing to Costa Rica Books, Suite 1 SJO 981, P.O.Box 025216, Miami Fl 33102-5216 or see the ad in Chapter 7.

Nicargaua has about 18,000 miles of roads of which 25% are paved. Travellers may drive legally in Nicaragua with a valid driver's license from their home country or an international drivers license.

To get a driver's license in Nicaragua, go to the local police station. You should technically be a resident to obtain a license and have a valid driver's license from your home country. An international driver's license will also work.

Whether you are renting a car or using your own automobile, always keep the proper documents in your car. Check with your lawyer to see what documents are required.

If a policeman should stop you, above all be polite, stay calm, and do not be verbally abusive. Most traffic police are courteous and helpful. However, if you commit a traffic violation, some policemen will try to have you pay for your ticket on the spot. Be advised this is not the standard procedure.

Be very careful when driving in Managua or any other cities. Many streets in Nicaragua are narrow, one-way and very crowded due to heavy traffic. When in doubt always yield the right of way. Some names of streets are not on sign posts on the street corners as in the United States. Some streets don't even have signs. Drive more slowly that you normally would in the States or Canada. Watch out for pedestrians as the often cross in the middle of the block.

Be aware of dangerous road conditions. When driving in

the countryside, drive only during the day, watch out for livestock, and be sure to use some kind of map. Don't get off the main paved road unless absolutely necessary during the rainy season if your car does not have four-wheel drive. You may end up getting stuck in the mud. Unfortunately, the only way to some of Nicaragua's best beaches is by unpaved roads. So be careful!

Be sure to familiarize yourself with traffic signs. If you get lost ask several people for directions. Often people will try to be friendly, but will give you the wrong directions with no malice in mind. Remember that many streets don't have names and most houses don't have numbers on the outside. Consequently, you'll have to learn how to navigate by using landmarks as refernces like the Nicaraguans do. Unfortunately, the landmarks given are not always familair to foreigners, so it is important to get the most complete directions as possible. Having a knowledge of Spanish will facilitate this process.

Travelling by boat is one way to get around Nicaragua.

Round Trip Back to Paradise
By Jay Trettien

"I never had more money or had more fun than when I lived in Costa Rica," was my response when a fellow bartender friend from southern California suggested we open a bar in Baja California.

"If you're heading South of the Border, you may as well go to Costa Rica, where the weather is nicer and the people more friendly," I said.

I was first invited to Costa Rica in 1973 by a college friend who worked for the Bank of America. Through the bank he had met an American who needed help with a bar he had just bought. My friend suggested that maybe I would come to Costa Rica to help out. A late-night phone call, and two weeks later I arrived from New York. After a few weeks of working together, the bar owner and I had developed trust and a friendship and, on the strength of a handshake, I became a partner in what was to become Central America's most popular "Gringo" rock and roll bar, Ye Pub. Gringos and ticos loved the place. After living in Costa Rica for a while, I was granted a cédula, or Costa Rican "green card."

But the time came to sell. Costa Rica had been enjoying a spectacular boom but, with small countries, as fast as it goes up, it can go down. After three years we sold.

With a girlfriend that was driving me nuts it was easy to leave Costa Rica. I visited every country in South America. I had already seen almost all of Europe, most of the United States and Canada. So, I ended up in Australia and New Zealand for about four years, finally washing up on the shores of southern California.

I began thinking about Costa Rica again and made a brief visit about 12 years ago to be pleasantly surprised that I still had friends in the country. I returned to California, loaded up the old Pontiac and ended up back in Costa Rica.

A lucky coincidence got me my cédula back when the Costa Rican government declared an amnesty for all foreigners, trying to get a grip on all the illegal Nicaraguans in the country.

Now I'm working at a popular San José hotel bar. I think I have about $150 under my mattress, but I have a good time and a lot of fun.

After visiting Granada, Nicaragua several times I've often thought if I were about ten or fifteen years younger, I'd definitely move to Nicaragua and start an expat bar.

I really like the atmosphere there. It kind of reminds me of Costa Rica about 20 years ago; a type of new frontier. Who knows? I may still end up there.

Distance in Kilometers

	MANAGUA	BLUEFIELDS	BOACO	CHINANDEGA	ESTELÍ	GRANADA	JINOTEGA	JINOTEPE	JUIGALPA	LEÓN	MASAYA	MATAGALPA	OCOTAL	PTO. CABEZAS	RIVAS	SAN CARLOS	SOMOTO
MANAGUA	0	383	88	132	148	45	162	46	139	93	29	130	226	557	111	300	216
BLUEFIELDS	383	0	322	510	462	402	476	422	243	476	386	444	540	842	461	351	530
BOACO	88	322	0	220	157	107	181	127	79	181	91	149	425	517	166	240	235
CHINANDEGA	132	510	220	0	161	177	194	177	271	37	161	181	238	591	243	43	229
ESTELÍ	148	462	157	161	0	166	103	185	219	141	151	71	78	498	226	383	68
GRANADA	45	402	107	177	166	0	180	41	184	138	16	148	244	576	68	318	234
JINOTEGA	162	476	181	194	103	180	0	202	232	175	165	32	181	459	240	377	171
JINOTEPE	46	422	127	177	185	41	202	0	202	122	37	170	266	603	65	346	256
JUIGALPA	139	243	79	271	219	184	232	202	0	229	141	198	296	599	208	160	297
LEÓN	93	476	181	37	141	138	175	122	229	0	122	130	219	650	187	394	209
MASAYA	29	386	91	161	151	16	165	37	141	122	0	130	229	558	73	301	219
MATAGALPA	130	444	149	181	71	148	32	170	198	130	130	0	149	297	297	343	139
OCOTAL	226	540	425	238	78	244	181	266	296	219	229	149	0	576	304	455	29
PTO. CABEZAS	557	842	517	591	498	576	459	603	599	650	558	428	576	0	625	760	566
RIVAS	111	461	166	243	226	68	240	65	208	187	73	297	304	625	0	318	244
SAN CARLOS	300	351	240	43	383	318	377	346	160	394	301	343	455	760	318	0	447
SOMOTO	216	530	235	229	68	234	171	256	297	209	219	139	29	566	244	447	0

To convert kilometers to miles, multiply by .6 which gives an approximate equivalent.

Travelling by Boat

Since the country's prominent geographical feature are its large lakes and rivers, boat travel is available. Boats are the only way to get to some places in Nicaragua, notably on the Caribbean coast and on Lake Nicaragua.

There is scheduled service on Lake Nicaragua. You can travel from Granada to Isla de Ometepe, and then on to San Carlos. There are also excursions by boat from Granda to some of the smaller islands in the lake. Isla de Ometepe may also be reached from San Jorge, near Rivas, in about an hour.

Trips down the Río San Juan del Norte are expensive.

Keeping Your Bearings Straight

You can get confused in Nicaragua, especially in Managua, trying to find your way around. Even though in Managua, Granada and León there are many streets which have names, It is more common to have an address given with reference to landmarks. People use known landmarks to get around, to locate addresses, and give directions.

In Managua it is especially hard to get around since many reference points were destroyed in the earthquake of 1972. If the word *"antiguo"* is used you can bet it refers to a landmark that stood before the earthquake. Also, it is important to always try and get as detailed instructions as possible since some landmarks given are not that familiar. For example, from the church three blocks arriba (east) and two blocks al lago (north).

If you are unfamiliar with this system it is almost impossible to find your way around, and easy to get lost. Don't worry, after you have lived in Nicaragua a while, you will get used to this system. In the event you get lost, you can always ask Nicaraguans for directions—provided you understand a little Spanish or they speak some English.

As you know, *Nicas* are generally very friendly and are usually happy to help you find the address you are looking for. However, it is always a good idea to ask a second person, because most Nicaraguans are embarassed to admit they don't know an address and will sometimes give you directions whether they know where you want to go or not.

Here is some important vocabulary which will help you find your way around Nicaragua. Many can be used outside of Managua as well. *Al lago* or *al norte* (north), *al sur* (south), (a couple blocks up or "east" in Managua), *abajo* or al *oeste* (a few blocks down or in Managua "west'), *una cuadra* or *100 varas* (one block), *barrio* or *reparto* (neighborhood), *colonia* (another word for neighborhood), *cuadra* (block), *antiguo* (refers to a place that is no longer standing), *pista* (highway or boulevard), *carretera* (a big highway), *costado* (the side of a block or square), *calle* (street), *esquina* (corner), *al frente* or *enfrente de* (in front of or across the street) *esquina* (corner), *diagonal* (diagonal to) and *contiguo* (next door to).

MORE USEFUL INFORMATION

Affordable Food

A wide variety of delicious tropical fruits and vegetables grow in Nicaragua. It is amazing that every fruit and vegetable you can think of besides some exotic native varieties flourish here. More common tropical fruits such as pineapples, mangoes and papayas cost about a third of what they do in the United States. Bananas can be purchased at any local fruit stand or street market for about five cents each. Some fruits and vegetables are imported from neighboring countries.

Supermarkets are much like markets in the U.S.; everything is under one roof, but the selection of products is smaller. However, don't expect to find the same variety and availability of products you do in a U.S. market. A lot of canned goods, packaged cereals and other products are imported from neighboring Costa Rica.

Nicaragugua's major supermarket chains are, **Palí, La Unión Supermercados** and **La Colonía Supermercados**. Palí is the largest with almost twenty markets in such places as

Managua, Granada, Masaya and Matagalpa.

In addition, there are thousands of small neighborhood corner grocery stores called *pulperías*. Also, many Shell gas stations have mini-markets as in the U.S.

Imported packaged products found in Nicaragua supermarkets are very expensive. It is usual to pay double for your favorite breakfast cereal, certain canned foods or liquor. Don't worry because there are some local products to substitute for your favorite U.S. brand. If you want to save money, we suggest you stock-up on these items on shopping trips to the States, in Costa Rica or Panamá and bring them back with you by plane.

Since foods are so affordable in Nicargaua, you will be better off changing your eating habits and buying more local products so you can keep your food bill low. You can save more money by shopping at any Central Market, **Mercado Central**, as many cost-conscious Nicaraguans do. Most cities

Modern U.S.-style supermarkets abound in Nicaragua.

Ceviche de Corvina
(Marinated White Seabass)

1 lb. seabass, cut in small pieces
3 tablespoons omion, finely chopped
1 tablespoon celery, finely chopped
2 tablespoons fresh coriander, chopped
2 cups lemon juice
Salt, pepper and Tabasco Sauce
1/2 teaspoon Worcester Sauce

Combine all ingredients in a glass bowl. Let it stand for at least four hours in the refrigerator.
Serve chilled in small bowls topped with catsup and soda crackers on the side. Serves 8.

TRES LECHES
(Three Milk Cake)

Cake Base
5 eggs
1 teaspoon baking powder
1 cup sugar
1/2 teaspoon vanilla
1 1/2 cups of flower
Preheat oven at 350 F. Sift baking powder. Set aside. Cream butter and sugar until fluffy. Add eggs and vanilla and beat well. Add flour to the butter mixture 2 tablespoons at a time, until well blended. Pour into greased rectangular Pyrex dish and bake at 350 F for 30 minutes. Let cool. Pierce with a fork and cover. For the filling combine 2 cups of milk, 1 can of condensed milk and one can of evaporated milk. Pour this mixture over the cool cake. To make the topping, mix 1 1/2 cups of half & half, 1 teaspoon vanilla and a cup of sugar. Whip together until thick. Spread over the top of the cake. Keep refrigerated. Serves 12.

and towns have some type of central market.

A few words about Nicaragua's excellent seafood. With oceans on both sides, a variety of fresh seafood is available. There are several varieties of fish as well as lobster and shrimp of all sizes . All of these can be purchased at any *pescadería* (fish market).

Typical Nicaraguan food is similar to that of Mexico and other Central American countries. Tortillas often, but not always, are eaten with a meal of rice, beans, fruit, eggs, vegetables and a little meat. *Gallo pinto*, a common dish, is made with rice and black beans as a base and fried with red bell peppers and cilantro. *Nacatamales* are a combination of meat, tomatoes, rice and condiments inside of a rectangular piece of corn meal. It is wrapped in banana leaves for cooking purposes.

Ceviche is raw fish marinated in lemon juice, onion and other spices (Please see the recipe we've included on the previous page). *Plátano Frito* are fried green plantains. *Vigorón* is a popular dish which consists of boiled yucca (cassava) topped with coleslaw salad and pork or *chicharrón* (fried pork

American fast food is available in Nicaragua.

MORE USEFUL INFORMATION

skins), served in a banana leaf.

The latter is sometimes called *toreja* by the locals. *Bajo* is another typical dish which has green plantains, yuca, meat and other vegetables. *Fritangas* are strips of fried vegetables.

Different kinds of natural fruit juice drinks are available uaually consisting of fruit, water and sugar. Major brand-name soft drinks, beer and some wines are availalbe. Street vendors sell drinks such as *posol con leche*, a corn and milk drink.

A wide variety of international cusine may be found in Managua's restaurants. **Los Antojitos** (222-7574) across from the Hotel Inter-Continental specializes in Mexican food. **Chopy Suey Internacional** (277-2340) and **Oriental Express** (265-1077) serve Chinese food and have home delivery. **El Mesón Español** (266-8561) has authentic Spainsh food. **La Marseillaise** (277-0224) is an excellent French restaurant. **Harry's Grill & Bar** (270-2382) is famous for it's meat dishes. **Rostipollos**, a Costa Rican chain, prepares delicious chicken cooked over coffee branches.

La Cocina de Doña Haydeé (270-6100) serves typical

Rostipollos offers the best chicken in Nicaragua.

Nicaraguan food.

Managua also has its share of American style fast food restaurants: **Pizza Hut, McDonald's, Pollo Supremo, Subway, Domino's Pizza** to name a few.

Granada has its share of good eateries but no fast food joints as of yet. American run **Hospedaje Central** has excellent affordable food. **Restaurante Doña Conchi's** serves Mediterranean cusine. Also try **Casa de Las Alemanas** for good food and drink. The **Nica Buffet** is famous for the best American breakfasts in town. **Terraza La Playa** is located at the edge of the lake.

Nicaragua's Holidays

Nicaraguans are very nationalistic and proudly celebrate their official holidays, called *feriados*. Plan your activities around these holidays and don't count on getting business of any kind done since most government and private offices will be closed. In fact, the whole country shuts down during *Semana Santa* (the week before Easter) and the week between Christmas and New Year's Days.

Nicaraguans love to celebrate holidays.

MORE USEFUL INFORMATION

January 1	New Year's Day*
Holy Week (Semana Santa)	Holy Thursday and Good Friday* These holidays vary every year
May 1	Labor Day (El día de trabajador)
July 19	Sandinista Revolution Day
August 1	Festival of Santo Domingo, Patron Saint of Managua
September 14	Anniversary of the Battle of San Jacinto
September 15	Independence of Central America
November 1	All Saints Day
November 2	The Day of the Dead (All Souls Day)
December 8	Immaculate Conception
December 25	Christmas Day*
December 31	New year's Eve

Religion

A large number of Nicaraguans are Roman Catholic, but there is freedom of religion and other religious views are permitted. Evangelical, Baptist and Pentocostal and Seventh Day Adventists are some of the other denominations.Like most Catholic countries in Latin America, Nicaragua has its calendar of Saint's Days or Santoral.

Churches and cathedrals are found all over the country.

Bringing Your Pet to Nicaragua

We did not forget those of you who have pets. There are procedures for bringing your pets into the country that require very little except patience, some paperwork and a small fee.

If you want to bring a pet into the country by land or air it is best to follow the following procedure to insure that there are no snags. First, a registered veterinarian from your home town must certify that your pets are free of internal and external parasites. It is advisible that your pet have up-to-date vaccinations against distemper, leptospirosis, hepatitis and parvovirus and a rabies vaccination within the last three years.

If the animal is traveling with you as part of your luggaage, the average rate is $50 US from one destination to the next (i.e. Los Angeles—Miami—San José). If your pet travels alone, depending on size and weight, the average rate is between $100 to $200 US. Please consult your airline for the actual price. Call the 800 toll-free cargo section of American Airlines and they will tell you the cost.

Whether your pet is traveling with you or separately, be aware that the weather can delay your animals arrival in Nicaragua. If the temperature is above 85 degrees or below 40 degrees at either your point of departure or a layover, your animal will not be able to travel. We know of several people who have arrived at the airport only to find out their animals could not travel due to a change in the weather. Call your airline the day you intend to ship your animal and again an hour or two before departure to see if your animal will be allowed to travel. This way you can avoid unpleasant surprises.

Also make sure your dog or cat has an airline approved portable kennel. These rules are very strict and the kennel must be the appropriate size for your animal or it won't be allowed to travel. Some airlines rent kennels. Make sure your kennel has a small tray so your pet can have food and water during the journey. Two to eight hours is a long time to go without food or water.

If there is a layover involved, as in Miami, the baggage handlers will give water to your pet. The operator at American Airlines told us about a special service which will walk your dog for an extra charge at some airports. Some people suggest tranquilizing dogs and cats when shipping them by plane. We talked to our vet when we were going to ship our large Siberian husky, and he didn't seem to think it was a good idea. We also asked a friend who ships show dogs all over the U.S. and he said to use our own judgement since tranquilizers can make an animal ill.

Additional information is available from a Nicaraguan consulate in the U.S. or Canada.

Most veterinarians offer the same services as in the U.S. or Canada surgery, neutering, shots, medicines, bathing of animals, haircuts, boarding, accessories and much more.

Veterinarians

Bosques de Altamira	278-2466
Clínica Veterinaria Dr. Solorzano.	222-3205
Centro Médico Veterinario	265-8601
Dr. Murillo	222-2279
Dr. Morazán	256-8269 or 265-8605

Understanding the Metric System

If you plan to live in Nicaragua, it is in your best interest to understand the metric system. You will soon notice that automobile speedometers, road mileage signs, the contents of bottles, and rulers are in metric measurements. Since you probably didn't study this system when you were in school and it is almost never used in the U.S., you could become confused.

The conversion guide below will help you.

To Convert:	To:	Multiply by:
Centigrade	Fahrenheit	1.8 then add 32
Square km	Square miles	0.3861
Square km	Acres	247.1
Meters	Yards	1.094
Meters	Feet	3.281
Liters	Pints	2.113
Liters	Gallons	0.2642
Kilometers	Miles	0.6214
Kilograms	Pounds	2.205
Hectares	Acres	2.471
Grams	Ounce	0.03527
Centimeter	Inches	0.3937

* *Courtesy of Central America Weekly.*

PARTING THOUGHTS AND ADVICE

Personal Safety in Nicaragua

Living in Nicaragua probably is much safer than residing in most large cities in the United States or many other Latin American countries, but you should take some precautions and use common sense to ensure your own safety. In Nicaragua, the rate for violent crimes is very low, but there is a problem with theft, especially in the larger cities. Make sure your residence has steel bars on both the windows and garage. The best bars are narrowly spaced, because some thieves use small children as accomplices as they can squeeze through the bars to burglarize your residence.

Make sure your neighborhood has a night watchman if you live in the city. Some male domestic employees are willing to work in this capacity. However, ask for references and closely screen any person you hire. Also, report suspicious people loitering around your premises. Thieves are very patient and often case a residence for a long time to observe your comings and goings. They can and will strike at the most opportune moment for them.

You should take added precautions if you live in an area where there are many foreigners. Thieves associate foreigners with wealth and look for areas where they cluster together. One possible deterrent, in addition to a night watchman, is to organize a neighborhood watch group in your area.

If you leave town, get a friend or other trustworthy person to house-sit.

Isolated areas offer tranquility but are less populated. This makes them prime targets for burglars and other thieves. This is the down side to living off-the-beaten-path.

If you own an automobile, Make sure your residence has a garage with iron bars so your car is off the street. When parking away from your house, always park in parking lots or where there is a watchman. He will look after your car for a few cents an hour when you park it on the street.

Never park your vehicle or walk in a poorly lit area. Avoid walking alone at night. You should never flaunt your wealth by wearing expensive jewelry or carrying cameras loosely around your neck because they make you an easy mark on the street. Keep a good watch on any valuable items you may be carrying. It is advisable to find a good way to conceal your money and never carry it in your back pocket. It is best to carry money in front pockets.

It is also a good idea to always carry small amounts of money in several places, rather than all your money in one place. If you carry large amounts of money, use traveler's checks. Be very discreet with your money. Don't flash large amounts of money in public. Every time you finish a transaction in a bank or store, put away all money in your purse or wallet before going out into the street.

Never carry any original documents, such as passports or visas. Make a photocopy of your passport and carry it with you at all times. The authorities will accept most photocopies

PARTING THOUGHTS AND ADVICE

as a valid form of identification.

Thieves often work in teams. One will distract you while the other makes off with your valuables. Never accept help from strangers, and ignore and never accept business propositions or other offers from people you encounter on the street. Never pick up hitchhikers.

Men should also watch out for prostitutes, who are often expert pickpockets and can relieve the unsuspecting of his valuables before he realizes it.

If you are a single woman living by yourself, never walk alone at night. If you do go out at night, be sure to take a taxi or have a friend go along.

White collar crime exists in every country and a few dishonest individuals—Americans, Canadians and Nicaraguans included—are always waiting to take your money. Scamsters prey off newcomers. One crook in Costa Rica bilked countless people out of their money by selling a series of non-existent gold mines here and abroad. The guy is still walking the streets today and dreaming up new ways to make money.

One "dangerous breed of animal" you may encounter are some foreigners between 30 and 60 years of age who are in business but don't have pensions. Most of said people are struggling to survive and have to really hustle to make a living . In general, they are desperate and will go to almost any means to make money. They may even have a legitimate business but most certainly try to take advantage of you to make a few extra dollars. Most complaints we hear about people being "ripped off" in Central America are caused by individuals who fit into this category.

Be wary of blue ribbon business deals seeming too good to be true, or any other get-rich quick schemes—non-existent land, fantastic sounding real estate projects, phony high-interest bank investments or property not belonging to the person selling it. If potential profit sounds too good to be true it probably is. Always check out the track record of an individual or company before you invest.

Always do your homework and talk to other expats before you make any type of investment. There seems to be something about the ambience here that causes one to trust total strangers. The secret is to be cautious without being afraid to invest. Before jumping into what seems to be a once-in-a-lifetime investment opportunity, ask yourself this question: Would I make the same investment in my home town? Don't do anything with your money in Nicaragua that you wouldn't do at home. A friend and long-time resident here always says jokingly when referring to the business logic of foreigners who come to Central America, "When they step off the plane they seem to go brain dead."

Most people in Nicaragua are honest, hard-working individuals. But don't assume people are honest just because they are nice. Remember, it doesn't hurt to be overly cautious.

Life As An Expatriate

Throughout this book we have provided the most up-to-date information available on living and retirement in Nicaragua. We have also provided many useful suggestions to make your life in Nicaragua more enjoyable and help you avoid inconveniences. Adjusting to a new culture can be difficult for some people. Our aim is to make this transition easier so you can enjoy all of the marvelous things that Nicaragua offers.

Before moving permanently to Nicaragua or any country, we highly recommend spending some time there on a trial basis to see if it is the place for you. We are talking about a couple of months or longer, so you can experience Nicaraguan

PARTING THOUGHTS AND ADVICE

life as it is. Remember visiting Nicaragua as a tourist is quite another thing from living there on a permanent basis. It is also good to visit for extended periods during both the wet and dry seasons, so you have an idea of what the country is like at all times of the year. During your visits, talk to many expats and gather as much information as possible before making your final decision. Get involved in as many activities as you can during your time in the country. This will help give you an idea of what the country is really like.

The final step in deciding if you want to make Nicaragua your home, is to try living there for at least a year. That's sufficient time to get an idea of what living in Nicaragua is really like and what problems may confront you while trying to adapt to living in a new culture. It will also let you adjust to the climate and new foods. You can learn all the dos and don'ts, ins and outs and places to go or places to avoid before making your final decision.

You may decide to try seasonal living for a few months a year. Many people spend the summer in the U.S. or Canada and the winter in Nicaragua (which is its summer), so they can enjoy the best of both worlds—the endless summer.

Whether you choose to reside in Nicaragua on a full or part-time basis, keep in mind the cultural differences and new customs. First, life in Nicaragua is very different. If you expect all things to be exactly as they are in the United States, you are deceiving yourself. The concept of time and punctuality are not important in Latin America. It is not unusual and not considered in bad taste for a person to arrive late for a business appointment or a dinner engagement. This custom can be incomprehensible and infuriating to North Americans, but will not change since it is a deeply-rooted tradition.

As we previously mentioned, in most cases bureaucracy moves at a snail's pace in Nicaragua, which can be equally maddening to a foreigner. In addition, the Latin mentality, machismo, apparent illogical reasoning, traditions, different laws and ways of doing business, may seem incomprehensible to a newcomer.

You will notice countless other different customs and cultural idiosyncrasies after living in Nicaragua for awhile. No matter how psychologically secure you are, some culture shock in the new living situation will confront you. The best thing to do is respect the different cultural values, be understanding and patient, and go with the flow. Learning Spanish will ease your way.

You should also read, *Survival Kit for Overseas Living* by L. Robert Kohls, Intercultural Press, P.O. Box 700, Yarmouth, Maine 04096. This guide is filled with useful information about adjusting to life abroad.

Nicaragua is an exciting place to live, but poses many obstacles for the newcomer. Don't expect everything to go smoothly at first or be perfect. By taking the advice we offer throughout this book, and adjusting to the many challenges, you should be able to enjoy all of Nicaragu's wonders.

Our recommendation is—don't burn your bridges or sever your ties with your home country; you may want to return home.

Finally, try taking the adaptability test on the next page to see if you are suited for living abroad.

PARTING THOUGHTS AND ADVICE

M.R.T.A. Overseas Living Adaptability Test

Using the figures 1 (below average), 2 (average) or 3 (above average), ask yourself the following questions and rate your answer accordingly. Couples should take the test separately. As you take the test, write your selected numbers down, then add them together. When completed, refer to the Score Comments Box at the bottom of this page.

1) Open to new adventures
    select one: 1 2 3
2) Flexible in your lifestyle
    select one: 1 2 3
3) Enthusiastic to new things in a new and different culture
    select one: 1 2 3
4) Able to make and enjoy new friends:
    select one: 1 2 3
5) Willing to learn at least basic phrases in a new language
    select one: 1 2 3
6) Healthy enough mentally and physically not to see family, friends and favorite doctor for occasional visits
    select one: 1 2 3
7) Confident enough to be in a "minority" position as a foreigner in a different culture
    select one: 1 2 3
8) Independent and self-confident enough not to be influenced by negative and often ignorant comments against a possible move to a foreign country
    select one: 1 2 3
9) Patient with a slower pace of life
    select one: 1 2 3
10) Usually optimistic
    select one: 1 2 3
11) Eager to travel to a new country
    select one: 1 2 3
12) Open mind to dealing with a different type of bureaucracy
    select one: 1 2 3
13) Understand enought to look at things in a different light without being critical and accepting the differences
    select one: 1 2 3
14) Financially stable without needing to work
    select one: 1 2 3

Score Comments:	
Your Score	Evaluation
37-45	Great move abroad
30--36	Will have a few problems
22-32	Some problems but possible
Less than 22	Forget it, stay home!

Courtesy of Opportunities Abroad. This test taken from the book "Mexico Retirement Travel Assistance." To order wrtie M.R.T.A., 6301 S. Squaw Valley Rd., Suite 23, Pahrump, NV 89648-7949

ADDITIONAL SOURCES OF INFORMATION ABOUT LIVING IN NICARAGUA

RELOCATION AND RETIREMENT CONSULTANTS have helped newcomers find success and happiness in Central America for over 15 years. They offer an extensive network of contacts and insider information for potential residents and investors. Their one-of a- kind tours to Costa Rica for potential investors and residents are excellent They now offering their services in Nicaragua. Christopher Howard leads all tours. Please see www.liveinnicaragua.com or www.liveincostarica.com or contact them at: Suite 1 SJO 981, P.O. Box 025216, Miami, FL 33102-5126, e-mail: crbooks@racsa.co.cr

TICO TRAVEL offers one-of-a-kind tours to Nicaragua. These trips are designed to introduce retirees, investors and entrepreneurs to the exciting opportunities that await them abroad. All trips are led by Christopher Howard, the author of this best-selling guidebook and renowned expert on living and doing business in Central America. Good news! They also offer shorter tailor-made tours for individuals, couples and small groups. Toll Free 800 493-8426 Fax (954) 493-8466 E-Mail: tico@gate.net, http: www.ticotravel.com.

Central America Weekly is a good way to keep up with what is going on in Nicaragua as well as the rest of Central America. It is available in bookstores, newsstands and hotels throughout Central America. To subscribe see Chapter 5.

PARTING THOUGHTS AND ADVICE

22 Things Every Prospective Expatriate Should Know by Shannon Roxborough

When moving to a foreign country, making adequate pre-departure preparations is essential. Here are some tips to make your international move easier.

1) Be sure to undergo a complete medical check-up before leaving to avoid dealing with a major health issue overseas.

2) Take one or more advance trips to your destination to familiarize yourself. It's worth the investment.

3) Take the appropriate documents on the advance trip to start the immigration paperwork. Consulate personnel in the country can secure the visa and residency permit more efficiently that those working thousands of miles away.

4) If you have dependent children, in your pre-departure research, be thorough in seeking the availibility of education in your host country.

5) Make sure you and your family understand the country's culture so that they know what will be accepted in terms of volunteer and leisure activities at your new home.

6) In case of emergencies, make sure you know good health-care providers and how to contact them.

7) Use a travel agency for booking en-route travel so you may search for low-cost fares.

8) Check into purchasing round-trip tickets for en-route travel. They may be less expensive that one-way. And the return may be used for other travel.

9) Remember the sale of your Stateside home increases tax cost due to lost interest deduction.

10) Cancel regular services and utilities. Pay the closing bill for garbage collecting, telephone, electricity, water, gas, cable TV, newspapers, magazines (or send them a change of address), memberships such as library and clubs, store accounts (or notify them that your account is inactive), and credit or check - cashing cards that will not be used.

11) Leave forwarding address with the Post Office or arrange for a mail forwarding service to handle all your U.S. mail.

12) Give notice to your landloard or make applicable arrangements for the sale of your home.

13) Have jewelry, art, or vaulables properly appraised, especially if they will be taken abroad. Register cameras, jewelery and other similar items with customs so that there will be no problem when reentering the U.S.

14) Make sure a detailed shipping inventory of household and personal effects is in the carry-on luggage and a copy is at home with a designated representative.
15) Obtain extra prescriptions in generic terms and include a sufficient supply of essential medicine with the luggage.
16) Obtain an international driver's liscense for all family members who drive. Some countries do not recognize an international driver's license but they issue one of their own, provided you have a valid home country license. Bring a supply of photographs as they may be required in the overseas location for driver's licenses and other identification cards.
16) Bring a notarized copy of your marriage certificate.
17) Arrange for someone to have power of attorney in case of an emergency.
18) Close your safety deposit box or leave your key with someone authorized to open it if necessary.
19) Notify Social Security Administration or corporate accounting department (for pensions) where to deposit any U.S. income. Make sure the bank account number is correct.
20) Bring copies of the children's school transcripts. If they are to take correspondence courses, make arrangements prior to departure and hand-carry the course material.
21) At least learn the Language basics prior to going to a foreign country. Trying to integrate with the new culture without the ability to communicate can be frustrating if not impossible.
22) Learn about the country's people and way of life before moving there. Go to your library, call your intended destination's tourism board and read all of the travel publications (magazines and travel guidebooks) you can to educate yourself.

Though this short article only provides a brief overview of the essentials, use it as a guide to prepare yourself for a smooth transition abroad.

Useful Resources:
Transitions Abroad Magazine 800 293-9373
A Guide to Living Abroad 609-924-9302

**Live in a beautiful tropical paradise for less than $ 30 a day, make money, enjoy the 'good life' and even find romance.
We've been doing it for years!
-Finds Out "How" in the #1 Best-selling
"The New Golden Door to Retirement and Living in Costa Rica".**

New 11th edition

"We highly recommend this guidebook to ALL of our members and to any anyone else thinking of living in Costa Rica. It is by far the BEST book on the subject. We have observed that people who read the book before coming here actually know MORE about the country than many long-term residents."
Debiem Gómez,
Residents Association of Costa Rica

You'll get all the insiders low down for living and investing in Costa Rica from this GREAT BOOK."
The Wall Street Journal

"This DOWN-TO-EARTH guidebook is filled with VALUABLE information and paints a clear picture of life in Costa Rica."
USA TODAY

ORDER TODAY!
Costa Rica Books
Suite 1 SJO 981, P.O. Box: 025216
Miami, Fl. 33102-5216
E-mail: crbooks@racsa.co.cr
or
www.costaricabooks.com
or
www.amazon.com

Price $ 24.95 U.S.D. ($3.00 per book shipping)

LiveInCostaRica.com

Live, Retire, Invest profitably, enjoy the good life and even find Romance for less than you ever Dreamed Possible.

We show you how to achieve your dream with all of the insider secrets and information, expert time-proven advice and a network of trustworthy contacts. We offer one-of-a-kind exploratory tours and consulting sessions for people of all ages interested in living, investing or retiring in Costa Rica.

Here is what people are saying about our services:

"Our tour was fabulous! Christopher Howard, our tour guide, mixed excellent information with lots of fun. His choice of speakers at the seminar gave my husband and I the sources we needed. Mr. Howard didn´t try to ´white-wash´ anything. Great! Great!

-María and Joseph JAcobs
Roanoke, VA

"After taking this fantastic, fact-filled tour all of the people in our group wanted to move to Costa Rica."

-Jim and Carol Burch
Cleveland, Ohio.

For more information or to book a tour contact us at:
E-mail: crbooks@racsa.co.cr
or
Call: 619 461-6131
Also see: www.liveincostarica.com

SUGGESTED READING

BOOKS

**Driving the Pan-American Highway to Mexico and Central America, by Raymond & Audrey Pritchard, $9.95. This is the only book available if you are planning to drive from the U.S. to Nicaragua via the Pan-American Highway. It is available from Costa Rica Books.

**Costa Rican Spanish Survival Course, by Christopher Howard. This one-of-a-kind book comes with a 90-minute cassette to accelerate the learning process. Also good for Nicaragua.

Nicaragua Guide, by Paul Glassman. Passport Press Box 1346, Chaplain, NY 12919 or from amazon.com. An excellent general overview of the country.

Nicaragua, by Carol Wood. Ulysses Travel Publications, 4176 Saint-Denis, Montréal, Québec H2W 2M5, Canada. The other travel guidebook dedicated solely to the subject.

Central America, a Lonely Planet Shoestring guide. Lonely Planet, 155 Filbert St., Suite 251, Oakland, CA 94607. This guide has a very complete section on Nicaragua.

Mexico and Central America Handbook. Passport Books, 4255 West Touhly Ave, Lincolnwood, Illinois 60646. This guide has a section of general information for the traveller.

Escape from America, by Roger Gallo. It is available from: http://www.escapeartist.com. This book is a must read for anyone who wants to relocate overseas. It has the answers to all of your questions. We recommend this book highly.

Guide to the Perfect Latin American Idiot, by Plinio Apuleyo Mendoza, Carlos Alberto Montaner and Alvaro Vargas Llosa. Madison Books, 4720 Boston Way, Lanham, Maryland 20706. This bestseller must be read by anyone in the United States or Canada who is interested in Latin America.

The International Man, by Douglas Casey. This book is the expatriate's bible to overseas living and investment. It is currently out of print, but you may be able to find it in a used bookstore or library.

The World's Retirement Havens, by Margret J. Goldsmith. This guide briefly covers the top retirement havens in the world. Most of the material is current since it was published in 1999. You may obtain this guide from John Muir Publications, P.O. Box 613, Santa Fe, New Mexico 87504.

How I Found Freedom in An Unfree World, by Harry Browne, Liam Works — Dept. FB, P.O. Box 2165, Great Falls, MT 59403-2165 or toll-free 1-888-377-0417. This book will revolutionize your life.

Living Overseas, What You Need to Know. This new guidebook promises to be good.

* Also access amazon.com. **They carry a full-line of titles about Nicaragua.**

PERIODICALS
Central America Weekly newspaper is published weekly. Packed with information about Central America as well as Nicarauga. See Chapter 4 to subscribe.

MOVIES
Under Fire, with Nick Nolte and Joanna Cassidy, paints a graphic of the fall of the Somoza regime.

Walker, by Alex Cox. A surrealistic picture.

****All of the titles above with a double asterisk **, are also available through Costa Rica Books' mail order catalog: Suite 1 SJO 981, P.O. Box 025216, Miami FL 33102-5216. To order directly, include $3.00 postage for the first book in the U.S. (Canada $4.00, Europe $5.00) and $1.00 for each additional book. Write for more details and a complete list of our other products and prices. You may call toll-free 619-461-6131 for more information. <u>You may also order our products through www.costaricabooks.com.</u>**

IMPORTANT SPANISH PHRASES AND VOCABULARY

You should know all of the vocabulary below if you plan to live in Costa Rica.

What's your name?	¿Cómo se llama usted?
Hello!	¡Hola!
Good Morning	Buenos días
Good Afternoon	Buenas tardes
Good night	Buenas noches
How much is it?	¿Cuánto es?
How much is it worth?	¿Cuánto vale?
I like	Me gusta
You like	Le gusta
Where is...?	¿Dónde está...?
Help!	¡Socorro!
What's the rate of exchange	¿Cuál es el tipo de cambio?

I'm sick	Estoy enfermo
where	dónde
what	qué
when	cuándo
how much	cuánto
how	cómo
which	cuál or cuáles
why	por qué
now	ahora
later	más tarde
tomorrow	mañana
tonight	esta noche
yesterday	ayer
day before yesterday	anteayer
day after tomorrow	pasado mañana
week	la semana
Sunday	domingo
Monday	lunes
Tuesday	martes
Wednesday	miércoles
Thursday	jueves
Friday	vienes
Saturday	sábado
month	mes
January	enero
February	febrero
March	marzo
April	abril
May	mayo

June	junio	tall	alto
July	julio	tired	cansado
August	agosto	bored	aburrido
September	septiembre	happy	contento
October	octubre	sad	triste
November	noviembre		
December	diciembre	expensive	caro
		cheap	barato
spring	primavera	more	más
summer	verano	less	menos
fall	otoño	inside	adentro
winter	invierno	outside	afuera
		good	bueno
north	norte	bad	malo
south	sur	slow	lento
east	este	fast	rápido
west	oeste	right	correcto
		wrong	equivocado
left	izquierda	full	lleno
right	derecha	empty	vacío
easy	fácil	early	temprano
difficult	difícil	late	tarde
big	grande	best	el mejor
small	pequeño, chiquito	worst	el peor
a lot	mucho	I understand	comprendo
a little	poco	I don't	
there	allí	understand	no comprendo
here	aquí	Do you speak	
nice, pretty	bonito	English?	¿Habla usted inglés?
ugly	feo		
old	viejo	hurry up!	¡apúrese!
young	joven	O.K.	está bien
fat	gordo	excuse me!	¡perdón!
thin	delgado	Watch out!	¡cuidado!

IMPORTANT VOCABULARY

English	Spanish	English	Spanish
open	abierto	waiter	el salonero
closed	cerrado	bill	la cuenta
occupied (in use)	ocupado	blue	azul
free (no cost)	gratis	green	verde
against the rules or law	prohibido	black	negro
		white	blanco
exit	la salida	red	rojo
entrance	la entrada	yellow	amarillo
stop	alto	pink	rosado
		orange	anaranjado
breakfast	el desayuno	brown	café, castaño
lunch	el almuerzo	purple	morado, púrpura
dinner	la cena		
cabin	la cabina		
bag	la bolsa	0	cero
sugar	el azúcar	1	uno
water	el agua	2	dos
coffee	el café	3	trés
street	la calle	4	cuatro
avenue	la avenida	5	cinco
beer	la cerveza	6	seis
market	el mercado	7	siete
ranch	la finca	8	ocho
doctor	el médico	9	nueve
egg	el huevo	10	diez
bread	el pan	11	once
meat	el carne	12	doce
milk	la leche	13	trece
fish	el pescado	14	catorce
ice cream	el helado	15	quince
salt	la sal	16	diez y seis
pepper	la pimienta	17	diez y siete
post office	el correo	18	diez y ocho
passport	pasaporte	19	diez y nueve

20	veinte	300	trescientos
30	treinta	400	cuatrocientos
40	cuarenta	500	quinientos
50	cincuenta	600	seiscientos
60	sesenta	700	setecientos
70	setenta	800	ochocientos
80	ochenta	900	novecientos
90	noventa	1000	mil
100	cien	1,000,000	un millón
200	doscientos		

* If you want to perfect your Spanish, we suggest you purchase our best-selling Spanish book, *"The Spanish Survival Course"*, and 90-minute cassette mentioned in Chapter 7. It is a one-of-a-kind pocket-sized course designed for people who want to learn to speak Spanish the Nicaraguan way.

IMPORTANT CONTACTS

(Contents: U.S. Embassy contacts, other U.S. government contacts, bilateral business councils, Nicaraguan government agencies, banks, market research firms, international financial institutions, trade and industry associations, local attorneys, real estate agents)

Department Of State
Chief, Economic/Commercial Section, Anthony Interlandi (starting 8/98)
Economic/Commercial Officer Isabella Detwiler (9/98)
Economic Officer Timothy Stater (8/98)
U.S. Embassy Managua
Unit 2703 Box 2
APO AA 34021
Tel: (505) 266-2291 or 266-6010, ext. 226; Fax: (505) 266-9056
E-mail: usbusiness@amemb.org.ni
Intenet: www.usia.gov/abtusia/posts/NU1/wwwhcom.html

Commercial Assistant
Javier Torres
U.S. Embassy Managua
Unit 2703 Box 2
APO AA 34021
Tel: (505) 266-6010, ext. 225; Fax: (505) 266-9056
E-mail: usbusiness@amemb.org.ni

U.S. Department of Agriculture/Foreign Agricultural Service (USDA/FAS)
Regional Agricultural Attaché Mr. Charles Bertsch U.S. Embassy San Jose
APO AA 34020
Tel: (506) 220-3939; Fax: (506) 232-7709

E-mail: bertschc@fas.usda.gov

Agricultural Assistant
Silvio Castellón
U.S. Embassy Managua
Unit 2703 Box 2
APO: AA 34021
Tel: (505) 266-6010, ext. 343; Fax: (505) 266-7006
E-mail: fasManagua@amemb.org.ni

Department of Commerce
Partnership Post Commercial Attaché Frank Foster
U.S. Embassy San José
APO AA 34020
Tel: (506) 220-2454; Fax: (506) 220-4783
E-mail: ffoster@doc.gov

Washington-based USG country contacts:

Department of State
Nicaragua Country Desk Officer David Alarid
ARA/CEN, Room 4915 Main State
Washington, DC 20520
Tel: (202) 647-1510; Fax: (202) 647-2597

Department of Commerce
Nicaragua Country Desk Officer Mark Siegelmann
Office of Latin America/Caribbean Basin Division
Room 3021 - 14th & Constitution Avenue NW
Washington, DC 20230
Tel: (202) 482-5680; Fax: (202) 482-4726
E-mail: siegelma@usita.gov

IMPORTANT CONTACT

USDOC Inter-American Development Bank Office
Commercial Liasion Officer Eric Weaver
Office Of The U.S. Executive Director
1300 New York Avenue, NW
Mail stop E0209
Washington, DC 20007
Tel: (202) 623-3821; Fax: (202) 623-2039

USDOC Latin American/Caribbean Business Development Center
Agribusiness Development Officer Thomas E. Wilde Jr.
U.S. Department Of Commerce, Room H3203
Washington, DC 20230
Tel: (202) 377-0703; Fax: (202) 377-2218
TPCC Trade Information Center, 1-800-USA-Trade

Department of The Treasury
Nicaragua Country Desk Officer Jeff Neil
15th & Pennsylvania Avenue
Room 5413
Washington, DC 20220
Tel: (202) 622-1268; Fax: (202) 622-1273

Overseas Private Investment Corporation (OPIC)
1100 New York Avenue NW
Washington, DC 20527
OPIC Finance: Tel: (202) 336-8581
OPIC Insurance: Tel: (202) 336-8525; Fax: (202) 408-9859

Export-Import Bank of the U.S.
Intl. Business Development Officer Robert S. Haight
811 Vermont Ave. NW
Washington, DC 20571
Tel: (202) 565-3919; Fax: (202) 565-3931

U.S. Customs Service
Attaché for Central America/Caribbean Ed Mederos
10800 Sunset Drive, Suite 380
Miami, FL 33173
Tel: (305) 596-6405; Fax: (305) 596-1973
Internet site: www.customs.ustreas.gov

U.S. Department Of Agriculture/Foreign Agricultural Service (USDA/FAS)
International Economist Leslie O'Connor
Western Europe & Inter-Americas Division (WEIAD)
Room 5524 Ag Bldg South
Washington, DC 20250
Tel: (202) 720-6010; Fax: (202) 690-2709
E-mail: oconnor@fas.usda.gov

U.S. Agricultural Trade Office, Western Hemisphere
William Westman
Stop 1080
1400 Independence Ave. S.W.
Washington, DC 20520-1080
Tel: (202) 720-3221, Fax: (202) 720-6063
E-mail: westman@fas.usda.gov

Amcham and Bilateral Business Councils:

Cámara de Comercio Americana de Nicaragua (Nicaraguan/American Chamber of Commerce)
President Adolfo Mcgregor
Executive Director: Desiree Pereira
Carretera Masaya, del Sandy's, 1c. abajo, Managua
Tel: (505) 267-3099, 267-3633; Fax: (505) 267-3098
Apartado Postal: 2720 Managua, Nicaragua
Email: amcham@ns.tmx.com.ni
Internet site: www.sgc.com.ni/amcham

IMPORTANT CONTACT

Nicaraguan American Chamber of Commerce in Miami
President Oscar Fonseca
444 Brickell Avenue, Suite 51-168
Miami, FL 33131
Tel: (305) 448-2495; Fax: (305) 375-0362

Assoc. of American Chambers Of Commerce in Latin America
President David Ivy
1615 H Street NW
Washington, DC 20062-2000
Tel: (202) 463-5485; Fax: (202) 463-3126

Nicaraguan Government Agencies

Ministerio de Agricultura y Ganadería (MAG)
(Ministry of Agriculture)
Minister Dr. Mario De Franco
Km 8-1/2 Carretera A Masaya, Managua
Tel: (505) 276-0233, 276-0235; Fax: (505) 276-0943

Ministerio de Construcción y Transporte (MCT)
(Ministry of Construction and Transportation)
Minister Ing. Edgar Quintana
Frente al Estadio Nacional, Managua
Tel: (505) 228-2061, 228-3698; Fax: (505) 228-2060

Ministerio de Economía y Desarrollo (MEDE)
(Ministry Of Economy and Development)
Minister Dr. Noel Sacasa
Frente Al Centro Comercial Camino de Oriente, Managua
Tel: (505) 267-0002, 267-0009; Fax: (505) 267-0041
Internet site: www.economia.gob.ni

Ministerio de Finanzas (MIFIN)
(Ministry of Finance)
Minister Ing. Esteban Duque Estrada
Frente a la Asamblea Nacional, Managua
Tel: (505) 228-7061, 228-1255; Fax: (505) 222-3033
Internet site: www.minfin.gob.ni

Ministerio de Salud
(Ministry of Health)
Minister Dr. Lombardo Martínez Cabezas
Complejo de Salud "Concepción Palacios", Managua
Tel: (505) 289-7811, 289-7164; Fax: (505) 289-7671

Banco Central de Nicaragua
(Central Bank of Nicaragua)
Minister-President Dr. Noel Ramírez
Edificio Banco Central, Managua
Tel: (505) 265-0460, 265-1843; Fax: (505-2) 265-2272
Internet site: www.bcn.gob.ni

Ministerio de Turismo (INTURISMO)
(Ministry of Tourism)
Minister Lic. Pedro Joaquín Chamorro
Antojitos 1 C. abajo y 1 C. al sur, Managua
Tel: (505) 228-1238, 228-1337; Fax: (505) 228-1187
Internet site: www.intur.gob.ni

Ministerio de Recursos Naturales (MARENA)
(Ministry of Natural Resources)
Minister Ing. Roberto Stadthagen
Km. 12-1/2 Carretera Norte, Managua
Tel: (505) 263-1273, 263-1271; Fax: (505) 263-1274

Telephone Company (ENITEL)

IMPORTANT CONTACT

Executive President, Ing. Pablo Ayón
Telcor Villa Fontana, Managua
Tel: (505) 278-4444 ext. 72100; Fax: (505) 278-8651

Telecommunications Regulator (TELCOR)
Director, Ing. Mario Montenegro
Entrada a Portezuelo, Managua
Tel: (505) 263-2171, ext. 400, Fax: 222-7328

Compañía Nicaragüense de Energía (ENEL)
(Electric Utility)
Minister, Ing. Octavio Salinas
ENEL Central, Managua
Tel: (505) 267-4103, 267-2688; Fax: (505) 267-4377

Instituto Nicaragüense de Energía (INE)
(Nicaraguan Energy Institute - Ministry of Energy)
Director Ing. Jaime Bonilla
INE Central, Managua
Tel: (505) 228-2057/58; Fax: (505) 222-7052
Internet site: www.ine.gob.ni

Corporación de Zona Francas
(Free Trade Zones Administration)
Executive President, Lic. Gilberto Wong
Km. 12-1/2 Carretera Norte, Managua
Tel: (505) 263-1530; Fax: (505) 263-1700

Mede-Pesca
(Fisheries Directorate of the Ministry of Economy and Development)
Executive President, Lic. Miguel Marenco
Km. 7 carretera sur, Managua
Tel: (505)265-0593; Fax: (505) 265-0590

Nicaraguan commercial banks
Banco de la Producción (BANPRO)
Gerente General Lic. Arturo Arana U.
Plaza Libertad, Contiguo a Metrocentro
Apartado 2309, Managua
Tel: (505) 278-2508; Fax: (505) 278-4113, 277-3996

Banco Nicaraguense de Industria y Comercio (BANIC)
Gerente General Lic. Orlando Castro
Centro Financiero Banic, Managua
Tel: (505) 267-2730; Fax: (505) 267-2127

Banco de Crédito Centroamericano (BANCENTRO)
Gerente General Ing. Julio Cárdenas
Edificio Bancentro
Km. 4-1/2 Carretera Masaya, Managua
Tel: (505) 278-2777; Fax: (505) 278-6001
Internet site: www.bancentro.com.ni

Banco de Exportación (BANEXPO)
Gerente General Ing. Adolfo Arguello
Centro Comercial Metrocentro, Managua
Tel: (505) 278-7171; Fax: (505) 277-3154
Internet site: www.banexpo.com.ni

Banco de América Central (BAC)
Gerente General Lic. Carlos Matus Tapia
Frente a Loteria Nacional
Apartado 2304, Managua
Tel: (505) 267-0220/3; Fax: (505) 267-0224

Banco Popular
Presidente Ejecutivo Ing. Gustavo Narvaez
Centro Comercial Nejapa, Managua
Tel: (505) 265-0331; Fax: (505) 265-1337

IMPORTANT CONTACT

Banco Mercantil (BAMER)
Gerente General Lic. Víctor Urcuyo
Plaza Banco Mercantil, Managua
Tel: (505) 266-8228/31; Fax: (505) 266-8024
Internet site: www.bancomer.nic.com

Banco Intercontinental (INTERBANK)
Gerente General Lic. José Felix Padilla
Semaforos Centroamerica, Managua
Tel: (505) 278-5959; Fax: (505) 278-3535 and 278-3537
Internet site: www.interbank-nic.com

Banco de Finanzas (BANFIN)
Gerente General Lic. Silvio Lanuza
Esquina Opuesta Hotel Intercontinental, Managua
Tel: (505) 222-2444; Fax: (505) 228-3056/7
Internet site: www.bcofinanzas.com.ni

Banco del Sur
Gerente General Ing. Edgar Pereira
Edificio Interplaza
Pista La Resistencia, Managua
Tel: (505) 278-1236/39; Fax: (505) 278-1242

Banco del Café de Nicaragua (BANCAFE)
Gerente General Lic. José Antonio Arias
Semaforos De Lozelza, Managua
Tel: (505) 278-4478, 278-4442; Fax: (505) 278-3461
Internet site: www.bancafe.com.ni

Banco Caley Dagnall
Gerente General Ing. Mauricio Pearson
Km. 3 Carretera Sur, Managua
Tel: (505) 268-0068; Fax: (505) 268-0069

Nicaraguan market research firms:

Grupo Empresarial Nicaraguense, S.A.
Director General Nelson Estrada Solórzano
Costado Sur Iglesia Las Sierritas de Sto. Domingo
Apdo 102-A, Managua
Tel: (505) 278-5013/14, 276-0556; Fax: (505) 276-0583

Cid/Gallup
Manager for Nicaragua and El Salvador, Sr. Federico Denton
Del Cartel, 2 C. Abajo, Carretera A Masaya, Managua
Tel: (505) 278-3132; Fax: (505) 278-1066

International financial institutions:

Inter-American Development Bank (IDB)
Resident Representative Martín Stabile
Km. 4-1/2 Carretera a Masaya
Apdo. 2412, Managua
Tel: (505-2) 267-0831 / 0832 / 0833; Fax: (505) 267-3469

International Monetary Fund (IMF)
Resident Representative José Gil-Díaz
Banco Central de Nicaragua
Km. 7 Carretera Sur, Managua
Tel: (505) 265-1843; Fax: (505) 265-1923

World Bank (IBRD)
Resident Representative Mr. Ulrich Lachler
Edificio Del Ministerio de Cooperación Externa, Managua
Tel: (505) 222-7089; Fax: (505) 222-3385

IMPORTANT CONTACT

Central American Bank for Economic Integration (CABEI / BCEI)
Resident Representative Róger Arteaga
Plaza España, Managua
Tel: (505) 266-4120; Fax: (505) 266-4143

Nicaraguan trade or industry associations in key sectors:

Centro de Exportaciones e Inversiones (CEI)
(Center for Exports and Investment)
Executive Director: Lic. María Hurtado De Vigil
Del Hotel Intercontinental, 2c. al sur, 1c. abajo, 1c. al sur,
Managua Tel: (505) 268-3860, 268-1064; Fax: (505) 268-1063
Internet: http://www.cei.org.ni

Cámara de Comercio de Nicaragua (CACONIC)
(Chamber of Commerce of Nicaragua)
President: Martín Bárcenas,
General Manager Lic. Manuel Bermúdez
Plaza España, 2c. al sur, 1/2c. arriba, Managua
Tel: (505) 268-3505, 268-3524; Fax: (505) 278-3600
E-mail: caconic@teledata.com.ni

Cámara de Industrias de Nicaragua (CADIN)
(Chamber of Industries of Nicaragua)
President: Enrique Salvo; Secretary: Dr. Gilberto Solís
De Los Semáforos de Plaza España 300 mts al sur, Managua
Tel: (505) 266-8847/51; Fax: (505) 266-1891

Asociación de Distribuidores de Productos de Consumo de Nicaragua (Association of Consumer Product Distributors)
General Manager: Lic. América de Urtecho
Km 4-1/2 Carretera Norte, Módulo 12, Oficentro Norte,
Managua Tel: (505) 249-0045, 249-0095; Fax: (505) 249-0079

Cámara de La Construcción de Nicaragua (Nicaraguan Chamber Of Construction)
President: Ing. Néstor Pereira
Colonia Mántica, Segundo Callejón No. 239, Managua
Tel: (505) 266-6525, 266-6528; Fax: (505) 266-2925

Cámara de La Pesca de Nicaragua (CAPENIC) (Fishing Chamber)
General Manager: Dr. Armando Segura
Camino de Oriente, Edificio B-2, Modulo A-6, Managua
Tel: (505) 278-7091, 277-0646; Fax: (505) 278-7054

Cámara Minera de Nicaragua (CAMINIC) (Mining Chamber)
Executive President: Frank Mena
Bo. Bolonia, de La Optica Nicaraguense 1c. abajo, Managua
Tel: (505) 266-8836; Fax: (505) 266-8753

Cámara de Firmas Nicaraguenses de Contadores Públicos y Consultores
President: Lic. Noel Cruz P.
Costado Sur de Telcor, Las Palmas, Managua
Tel: (505) 266-0066; Fax: (505) 266-2347
Apartado Postal No. 2077, Managua, Nicaragua

Consejo Superior de La Empresa Privada (COSEP) (High Council for Private Enterprise)
President Ing. Gerardo Salinas, Executive Director: Dr. Orestes Romero Rojas
Telcor Zacarías Guerra 175 mts abajo, Managua
Tel: (505) 228-2030/40; Fax: (505) 228-2041
Apartado Postal No. 5430, Managua, Nicaragua

IMPORTANT CONTACT

Comité Nacional de Productores de Azúcar (CNPA)
(National Sugar Producers Committee)
General Manager: Lic. Noel Chamorro
Sandy's Carretera a Masaya 1 c. arriba 1 c. al sur, Casa #51, Colonial Los Robles
Apartado Postal No. A-223, Managua
Tel: (505) 267-8202, 277-5447; Fax: (505) 267-0197

Unión de Productores Agropecuarios de Nicaragua (UPANIC)
(National Unión of Agricultural Producers)
Executive Secretary: Ing. Alejandro Raskosky
Reparto San Juan No. 300, detrás del Ginmasio Hércules, Managua
Tel: (505) 278-3382/84; Fax: (505) 278-2587, 278-3291

Asociación Nicaragüense de Productores y Exportadores de Productos No-Tradicionales (APENN)
(Association of Producers And Exporters of Non-Traditional Products)
General Manager: Lic. Mario Amador Rivas
Hotel Intercontinental 2 c. al sur 2 c. al oeste, Managua
Tel: (505) 222-7063, 222-7067/8, 266-5038; Fax: (505) 266-5039

Cámara Nacional de Turismo
(National Chamber of Tourism)
Executive Director: Dr. Mario Medrano
Contiguo al Ministerio de Turismo, Managua
Tel: (505) 266-5071; Fax: (505) 266-5071

Federación de Asociaciones de Ganaderos de Nicaragua (FAGANIC) (Federation Of Nicaraguan Cattle Associations)
President: Ing. Juan Jose Roa
Entrada Principal, Centro Comercial Managua
Tel: (505) 277-2976, 277-2947; Fax: (505) 267-0084

Asociacion Nicaraguense de Formuladores y Distribuidores de Agroquimicos (ANIFODA) (Nicaraguan Association of Agrochemical Blenders and Distributors)
Executive Secretary: Dr. Salvador Borgen
P.O. Box 2067, Managua

Asociación de Bancos Privados de Nicaragua (ASOBANP) (Private Banking Association)
Executive Secretary: Dr. Francisco Ortega
Distribuidora Vicky 1 C. al sur 1 C. arriba, No. 235, Managua
Tel: (505) 278-3821; Fax: (505) 278-3820

Unión Nicaraguense de Pequeña y Mediana Empresas (UNIPYME) (Small and Mid-Sized Business Association)
President: Lic. Rafael Solórzano Dávila
Ciudad Jardín L-16, Managua
Apartado Postal No. 115, Managua
Tel: (505) 249-7695; Fax: (505) 249-0662

Confederación de Asociaciones Profesionales de Nicaragua (CONAPRO) (Confederation of Professional Associations)
President: Dr. Carlos Bayardo Romero
Canal 2 1 c. al sur 150 vrs. al oeste, Managua
Tel: (505) 266-4065, 266-2349, Fax: (505) 266-4650

Instituto Nicaraguense de Desarrollo (INDE)(Nicaraguan Development Institute)
President: Ing. William Baez
Camas Lunas 1 C. al oeste, Calle 27 De Mayo, Managua
Apartado Postal No. 2598, Managua
Telefax: (505) 268-1900/1.

IMPORTANT CONTACT

Asociación Nicaraguense de Ingenieros y Arquitectos (ANIA)(Association of Architects and Engineers)
President: Arq. Donald Flores Soto
Apartado Postal No. 1408, Managua
Tel: (505) 249-8177/8

Cámara Nacional De La Mediana Y Pequeña Industria (CONAPI) (Small and Mid-Sized Industries Chamber)
President: Antonio Chávez
Centro de Exposiciones La Piñata, Managua
Tel: (505) 278-4892, 277-5910

Nicaraguan attorney list:

The author does not guarantee the professional ability or integrity of the persons on this list. Their names are arranged alphabetically. All reside in Managua, speak English, and are public notaries. An asterisk following the name indicates the attorney has registered his/her signature at the U.S. consulate, facilitating the authentication of local documents for use in the U.S.

Gloria Alvarado and Associates
Industrial property law, commercial law, banking law, international law/foreign investment,
privatization, real estate, labor law, environmental law, commercial litigation
Del Lacmiel, 5c. arriba, 300 mts a la derecha, no. 75
Tel: 505-277-4028 and 278-7708; Fax: 505-278-7491
E-mail: alvasoc@ns.tmx.com.ni
Internet site: www.lexmundi.org/052.html

Emilio Barrios and Associates (*)
Corporate law, international banking, business law, patents,

trademarks, and civil litigation
Detrás del Restaurante La Marsellaise, 1c. abajo
Tel: 505-278-0019; Fax: 505-278-6576
E-mail: barrios@ibw.com.ni

Guy José Bendaña-Guerrero and Associates
Intellectual property law, chemical patents, license negotiation, industry models, trade marks,
patents, pharmaceutical patents, general intellectual property practice.
Porton Antiguo Hospital El Retiro, 1c. al lago
Tel: 505-266-5696 and 266-5697; Fax: 505-266-8863
E-mail: guybengu@ibw.com.ni

Francisco José Boza Páiz and Associates (*)
Business, fiscal and banking law
Parque Las Madres 1 C. al lago, Casa No. 1603
Tel: 505-266-8860 and 266-2374; Fax: 505-266-2374
Terencio García of Mayorga, Valdivia, Rivas, and Escobar
Corporate law, finance
Apartado Postal 2536, Managua
Tel: 505-268-2233; Fax: 505-268-2234

López Arguello, Morales & Associates
Patent and trade marks, foreign investment, banking, customs, foreign trade, real estate
corporations, administrative, commercial, civil, labor and tax law, oil and mineral, agency and
distribution agreements, insurance, litigation and arbitration
Canal 2, 300 vrs al oeste, 25 mts al sur
Tel: 505-266-0803 and 268-3070; Fax: 505-268-0017

Alvaro Martínez Cuenca
General practice, trademarks and patents

IMPORTANT CONTACT

Centro Comercial San Francisco, H-5
Tel: 505-278-0330; Fax: 505-277-1032
E-mail: ccisa@sgc.com.ni internet site: sgc.com.ni/ccisa

Juan Alvaro Munguía A., Luis Chávez Escoto and Associates
Banking and security law, general corp., Commercial law, leasing and project finance, foreign investment, mergers and acquisitions, private and administrative law, telecommunications, mining/oil/gas. environmental, intellectual property and technological law, labor law, litigation and arbitration bankruptcy/and shipping law, taxation and customs law, real estate law.
Edificio Málaga, Plaza España (2nd Floor)
Tel: 505 266-4157 and 266-1211; Fax: 505 266-4156
e-mail: jmunguia@ibw.com.ni; Internet site: www.lexmundi.org

Nicaraguan Real Estate Firms:

Bienes Raíces Alpha, S.A.
Las Palmas detrás de Telcor, Managua
Telefax: 505-266-5678

Bienes Raíces Sotelo & Novoa, S.A.
Cine Altamira, 2 1/2c. abajo, #437, Managua
Tel: 505-277-3401; Fax: 505-278-2790

Blandón Bienes Raíces
Sandy's Carretera a Masaya, 2c. arriba, #76, Managua
Tel: 505-278-5306; Fax: 505-278-0045

González Pasos Bienes Raíces
Parque Las Palmas, 1/2c. al oeste, Managua
Apartado Postal 2130, Managua
Tel: 505-266-8910; Fax: 505-266-1002

E-mail: gonpasos@ibw.com.ni,
internet: www.gonzalezpasosrealtors.com/

Rappaccioli International Investment, S.A.
Telefax: 305-665-2187 (Miami), 505-266-6763
Real Team Bienes Raíces, S.A.
Sandy's Carretera a Masaya, 2c. arriba, 20 vrs. al lago, Managua
Tel: 505-278-2676; Fax: 505-278-2657

Re/Max Nicaragua
General Manager Marcos Menocal
Calle El Arsenal, #305, Granada
Telefax: 505-552-3009

Sniders Realty
P.O. Box 3931, Managua
Tel: 505-278-3230; Telefax: 505-552-4702
E-mail: srealty@ibw.com.ni, internet: www.ibw.com.ni/~srealty

*Courtesy of U.S. Embassy Managua Econ/Commercial Section
.Home Page usembassy.state.gov/posts/nu1/wwwhcom.html

IMPORTANT TELEPHONE NUMBERS

MANAGUA
AUGUSTO SANDINO. ....505) 233-1624
INTERNATIONAL AIRPORT
IMMIGRATION ....(505) 339-9456
POLICE..118
TRAFFIC POLICE...119
FIRE 115
ENITEL...112
AMBULANCE 265-2086
RED CROSS .... 128 or 265-1761
HOSPITAL BAUTISTA 249-7070
HOSPITAL ALEMAN NICARAGUENSE................249-0701
HOSPITAL BERTHA CALDERON..........................260-1787
HOSPITAL MANOLO MORALES 277-0990
HOSPITAL ALEJANDRO BOLANOS.....................222-2765
HOTEL CAMINO REAL 263-1381
HOTEL INTERCONTINENTAL 228-3530
HOTEL PRINCESS 270-2574
HOTEL LAS MERCEDES 223-2111
HOTEL LAS PALMAS 266-6885
TAXI ....222-7937, 249-4669 or 222-5218

GRANADA
FIRE 552-4020
POLICE...118 or 552-2929
TRAFFIC POLICE 552-4578
AMBULANCE 119
HOSPITAL...552-7049 or 552-2719
JAPANESE HOSPITAL...552-7049
POLICLINIC 552-5854
TAXI........................... 552-4699, 552-4980 or 552-3092
ENITEL ....552-2032 or 552-2150
RED CROSS 552-2711
POST OFFICE..552-3311

HOSPEDAJE COCIBOLCA 552-2676
HOTEL ALHAMBRA 552-4486
POSADA HOTEL DON ALFREDO (hotel/bar) 552-4455
ESFINGE DON ALFREDO'S (hotel) 552-4826
HOTEL COLONIAL 552-7299
INTERBET SERVICES 552-3368
CASA INTERNACIONAL JOXI...............................458-2348

MONTELIMAR
HOTEL BARCELO MONTELIMAR 78-2572

LEON
HOSPITAL. 311-3566
RED CROSS..311-2135
POLICE 311-3137
TRAFFIC POLICE..311-3275

MASAYA
RED CROSS..522-2330
ENITEL 552-2032
POLICE 522-4222
FIRE 522-2313
HOSPITAL 522-2778, 522-2313
HOTEL CAILAGUA 522-4435

SAN JOAUN DEL SUR
RED CROSS..0283-0234
HOSPITAL..0283-0238
ENITEL 0283-0366
GUEST HOUSE (hotel) SODA ELIZABETH 0458-2270
MARIE'S BAR AND RESTAURANT 045-82-555

MATAGALPA
RED CROSS..612-2059
HOSPITAL..612-2081
POLICE. 612-2381, 62122382
FIRE. 612-3167

IMPORTANT TELEPHONE NUMBERS

ENITEL 612-3460

ESTELI
RED CROSS..713-2330
HOSPITAL..713-2439
FIRE. 713-2413
POLICE 713-2615

RIVAS
RED CROSS..453-3415
HOSPITAL...453-3011, 453-3301
FIRE 453-3511
POLICE 453-3732
ENITEL 453-3577

CHINANDEGA
RED CROSS..341-3132
HOSPITAL..341-4092
FIRE. 341-3221
POLICE 341-3456
ENItEL...341-2037

JINOTEGA
RED CROSS..632-2222
HOSPITAL..632-2626
FIRE 632-2468
POLICE ....118 or 632-2626, 632-02215
ENItEL...632-2261

BLUEFIELDS
RED CROSS..822-2582
HOSPITAL..822-2621
FIRE 822-2298
POLICE 822-2448

INDEX

A
Accidents, 178
Activities, 125-148
Aguinaldo, 40
Ahorita, 103
Airlines, 171
Ambulance, 227-229
Airport, 171
American Chamber of Commerce, 212
American Embassy, 121
American Legion, 138
Apartados, 153

B
Banks, 51
Baseball, 137
Beaches, (Playas),
    Casares, 15
    ElAstillero, 15
    El Tránsito, 15
    El Velero, 15
    Huehuete,15
    Jiquilillo, 15
    La Boquita, 15
    Montelimar, 15
    Pochomil, 15
    Poneloya, 15
    Salinas Grande, 15
    San Juan del Sur, 15
Bearings, 181
Bicycling, 133
Birds, 133
Birdwatching, 133
Bluefields, 229
Books, 203
Budget, 30

Bureacracy, 101
Burglary, 194
Buses, 172
Butterflies,

C
Cable TV, 128
Car Insurance, 65
Car Rentals, 176
Casinos, 147
Catarina, 12
Central Market, 184
Ceviche, 185
Chamorro, 20
Charter Flights, 171
Chinandega, 229
Churches, 189
Citizenship, 112
Climate, 5
Clínica Bíblica, 46
Clínica, 46
Clubs, 138-139
Colleges, 166
Companionship, 139
Con Men, 195
Continental Airlines, 172
Contras, 20
Córdoba, 50
Correo, 152
Cost of Living, 31
Country Clubs, 133
Crime, 193
Currency, 50

D
Dancing, 145

INDEX

Darío, Rubén, 13
Democracy, 21
Dental Care, 47
Discotheques, 145
Driving In Nicaragua, 177
Driver's License, 177

E

Earthquake, 19
Economy, 21
Embassies Abroad, 122
Embassies in Nicaragua, 121
Emergency Medical Services, 45-46, 227-230
Enitel, 149
Estelí, 14
Exchange Rates, 50
Exit Visas, 111-112
Extending Tourist Cards, 111-112

F

Farmacia, 48
Fast Foods, 186-187
Feriados, 188
Finding A Lawyer, 117
Finding Work, 89
Fire Department, 227-229
Fish, 186
Fishing, 136
Food, 183

G

Gallo Pinto, 186
Gambling, 147
Geography, 1
Government, 21
Granada, 8
Gravámenes, 86

Gyms, 134

H

Health Care, 44
Hired Help, 33
Holidays, 188
Honorarios, 118
Hospitals, 45-46

I

Independence, 19
Insurance, 65
International Telephone Calls, 150
Investments, 67

J

Jinotega, 229
Jiquilillo, 15
Jogging, 133

K

Keeping Busy, 125

L

Lake Apoyo, 12
(La Laguna de Apoyo),
Lake Managua, 6
(El Lago de Managua),
Lake Nicaragua, 1, 6
(Lago de Nicaragua)
LASCA, 172
La Prensa, 115
Lawyers, 119-120, 223-225

Leaving the Country, 111
Legal Advice, 117
León, 13
License, Driver's, 177
Lista de Correos, 153
Long Distance, 149-150

M

Machismo, 26
Magazines, 126
Making Friends, 138
Maids, 33
Mail, 152-153
Maps, 3, 4, 7
Markets, 183-184
Masaya, 12
Masaya Volcano, 12
Matagalpa, 14
Medical Care, 44
Medicine, 48
Meeting Places, 138-139
Money, 50
Money, Sending, 154
Montelimar, 15
Movie Theaters, 147
Museums, 134
Music, 145

N

Newspaper,
    English Language, 126
Nicaragua, 1-134
Nightlife, 145

O

Ometepec, 16
Ortega, Daniel, 20
Outdoor Activities, 133, 135

P

Pensionado, 104, 106
People, 23
Pets, 189
Pharmacies, 48
Plastic Surgery, 49
Playas (see beaches), 15
Pochomil, 15
Police, 177, 227-229
Post Office, 152
Pre-Schools, 167
Private Universities, 166
Prostitution, 141
Provinces, 121
Public Universities, 166
Pulperías, 184

Q

Quetzal, 16

R

Rain, 5
Real Estate, 80
Red Tape, 101
Religion, 189
Rentals, 81
Requirements for Pensionado
    Status, 103-110
Residency, 103
Restaurants, 187
Roads, 177
Romance, 139

S

Safety, 193

INDEX

Samoza, 19
Sandinistas, 20
San Juan del Sur, 15
Schools
    Bilingual private, 167
    Spanish, 163
Shipping Companies, 114
Shipping Your Household
    Goods, 113
Shopping, 130
Social Security, 102
Spanish, 157
Spanish Survival Course, 161
Sports, 133, 135, 137
Sport Fishing, 135
Street-numbering System, 181
Supermarkets, 183
Surfing, 136
Swimming, 135-136

T

Taxes, 52, 59
Taxis, 174
Telephone Service, 149
Tennis, 133
Theater,
Tourism,147
Tourist Visas, 112
Traffic, 177

U

United Airlines, 172
Universities, 166
University Study Programs, 166
U.S. Embassy, 121

V

Veterinarians, 191

Video Rentals, 130
Visas, 111
Vos, 163

W

Walker, William, 19
Watchman, 194
Water, Drinking, 44
Water Sports, 136
Weather, 3
Weight Lifting, 134
Wind Surfing, 136
Work, 89

Y

Yucca, 186

Z

Zelaya, 19

NOTES

pacific alliance marketing grp.
389-
(PMG.)